MODERN LEGAL STUDIES

SETTLEMENTS OF LAND

MODERN LEGAL STUDIES

SETTLEMENTS OF LAND

by
BRIAN W. HARVEY, M.A., LL.B. (Cantab.)

Professor of Property Law at the University of Birmingham;
Associate of the Institute of Taxation;
Solicitor of the Supreme Court

SWEET & MAXWELL
1973

Published in 1973 by
Sweet & Maxwell Limited of
11 New Fetter Lane, London
and printed in Great Britain
by Northumberland Press Limited
Gateshead, Co. Durham

SBN   Hardback 421 17090 5
      Paperback 421 17100 6

CONTENTS

OTHER BOOKS IN THE SERIES:

GENERAL PREFACE TO MODERN LEGAL STUDIES

MODERN LEGAL STUDIES is a series written for students of law in Universities, Polytechnics, and other institutions of higher education. It originated in the belief that law students need a series of short, scholarly monographs in different areas of the law, resembling those now being produced in other fields of social science.

The Series has five principal aims. First, it aims to supplement traditional textbooks by providing opportunity both for new topics to be written about and introduced into the syllabus of traditional courses, and for older topics to be given deeper consideration than they receive in the standard texts. Secondly, as the series progresses, it aims to provide a possible alternative to the one-textbook-per-course approach of many law courses; a set of several short books in, for instance, Property Law, could be used as substitutes for the present all-purpose texts. This would enable the student to become acquainted with a variety of views and approaches to the subject. Thirdly, the existence of a series of small, relatively cheap, legal monographs will, it is hoped, facilitate the breaking of boundaries between traditional courses—*e.g.* Contract and Tort,—and the creation of new courses built upon monographs in the Series.

Fourthly, the Series aims to promote greater consideration on the part of other social scientists of the legal aspects of social political and economic problems who are too often discouraged from considering the law on a whole range of matters because of the daunting nature of legal textbooks. Without compromising on the standards of legal scholarship, a smaller monograph should prove less formidable and therefore more useable. Fifthly, and by no means least in importance, the Series offers an outlet to legal scholars in the

vii

United Kingdom and elsewhere. The Editorial Board hopes that, where they have something worth saying to a wider audience than their own students, but which does not fit the length of either a law review article or a full-length book, they will be stimulated to prepare a monograph for the Series.

Modern Legal Studies then has ambitious aims, which will be realised only with time. But it is very much a co-operative venture, between the authors, who have written or are writing for the Series, the Editorial Board, and the wider community of legal scholars, teachers and students who are both the consumers now and, it is hoped, the producers of the future.

J. P. W. B. McAuslan
University of Warwick

PREFACE

THE author's preface is rather like the defendant's statement in mitigation from the dock—an admitted offence has occurred but at least (so the defendant thinks) the magistracy should have the opportunity of hearing the irresistible reasons which made its commission inevitable.

First, a negative statement. This comparatively short work is not intended to be a minute examination of the substantive law of conveyancing relating to settlements of land. Students of English law are fortunate in having a number of standard textbooks which already serve this purpose admirably. My debt to these is manifest and there are a number of references for instance, to the latest editions of Megarry and Wade, Cheshire and the Casebook of Maudsley and Burn in particular, in the text. Most students will have access to these texts and to regurgitate this material would be futile.

I have, therefore, attempted to do something rather different. Instead of drawing a detailed ordinance survey map of the substantive law I have tried to present something more resembling an aerial photograph of the topography of the subject which at the same time brings into greater relief modern features, particularly taxation, which are easily lost or are absent entirely in the traditionally drawn ordinance survey map.

I have also tried to give much greater emphasis to the basic skills of draftmanship, legislative and private, than is usual. So, as regards what the legislation concerning settled land attempts to do, I have analysed this first by presenting the problem in its historical context and then, looking through the eyes of the legislative draftsman, have tried to explain what devices he decided to use in an attempt to solve the problems. The case law is then examined in some detail, but again, the emphasis is on such cases as tend to show up the flaws in the architectural design.

I have been privileged to have been a member of the Northern Ireland Land Law Working Party which published (H.M.S.O. 1971, "Survey of Northern Ireland Land Law") and presented to the director of Law Reform a complete redraft of the English "Birkenhead" legislation. Having been primarily responsible for (*inter alia*) the redraft of the settlements provisions I soon became very conscious of the intellectual challenge of this type of venture and its educational value. The legislative draftsman, after all, merely performs at a more advanced level the function which most solicitors and a good many barristers perform as a routine task, namely the solution of present or predicted problems by a carefully drafted document of some kind agreed to by the parties. Litigation is not involved unless the arrangement completely breaks down. I hope, therefore, by stressing the "non-pathological" side of lawyers' operations it may encourage others, too, to promote a more realistic understanding of the essentially non-contentious work of most lawyers and the thought processes which are involved in this way of working. With regard to draftsmanship at the level of conveyancing in private practice, I have included as many examples of this in its fiscal and non-fiscal role as the length of the book allows.

Readers will find a number of references to pre-1926 position, a feature which I recognise to be unfashionable. I am unrepentant, partly because the modern law of settlements of land cannot be understood without some knowledge of the pre-1926 position, and partly also because the book has a comparative law slant. Consequently I hope it may be found of use in some of the many common law jurisdictions, which begin as near as Ireland, and which have not enacted anything similar to the Settled Land Act 1925 or the Law of Property Act 1925.

The current importance of the topic stems largely from fiscal considerations, as I try to make clear. It is perhaps to be deplored that this should be so. In the USA, for instance, one would highlight quite a different feature of the law of future interests since that country's fiscal structure happens to favour the taxpayer who creates successive life interests.

In the United Kingdom this is not so, subject to some important exceptions. In the case of either country, the devices used by conveyancers over the centuries have been retained or rejected not necessarily because of their inherent unsuitability but because of their fiscal consequences. But we must now accept the realities of the situation and colour the way so as to show the approved bridlepaths through the wood. Again, my debt in this respect to the standard works on taxation, particularly Pinson's *Revenue Law*, Potter and Monroe's *Tax Planning* and Morcom's *Estate Duty Saving*, is great. I hope that the end product will be of interest to law students making an advanced study of land law and also to practitioners who wish to consider some ideas for the employment of settlements.

I should also like to thank specifically or generically a number of people and organisations. First, my colleagues of the Land Law Working Party, my students at Belfast who asked some embarrassingly good questions, the General Editor for commenting constructively on the draft, the publishers for their co-operation and the Queen's University of Belfast for helping with research facilities. I also received material help from Mr. Robert Roper of H.M. Land Registry, the Law Commission and various other institutions and individuals including the fellow solicitors with whom I have worked. I alone am responsible for any mistakes or shortcomings. Finally I gratefully acknowledge my wife's encouragement and help with the tables.

The law is stated as in March 1973 and I have attempted to incorporate the main provisions of the Budget 1973 into the text.

BRIAN HARVEY

The University of Birmingham

TABLE OF CASES

TABLE OF STATUTES

"I cannot bear to think that they should have this estate. If it was not for the entail I should not mind it."

"What should you not mind?"

"I should not mind any thing at all."

"Let us be thankful that you are preserved from a state of such insensibility."

"I never can be thankful, Mr. Bennet, for any thing about the entail. How any one could have the conscience to entail away an estate from one's own daughters I cannot understand, and all for the sake of Mr. Collins too!—Why should *he* have more than anybody else?"

"I leave it to yourself to determine," said Mr. Bennet.

Pride and Prejudice—Jane Austen.

Chapter 1

WHY SETTLEMENTS?

WHY do people wish to settle land so as to control the way it (1)
is used by future generations? The answer to this question is
only partly supplied by reference to the cold legal and fiscal
consequences that follow from a settlement and in any event
would vary according to the century about which the question
was asked. Sentiment, the idea that it was desirable to be
able to say on one's deathbed "te teneam moriens," has
always played a part. It is also indisputable that until comparatively recently, the desire to settle land was closely connected with the political power which was accorded to the
large landowner. The basis of the parliamentary franchise was
from early times the ownership of land. In 1430 the franchise
was given in county elections to freeholders having tenements
of the annual value of forty shillings, and this in substance
continued until the enfranchisement in 1832 of copyholders,
tenants holding under leases for various periods, and tenants-
at-will paying rent of not less than £50. More important still,
from early times shire members of the House of Commons
were required to be "notable esquires and gentlemen," a
requirement initially stemming from usage but buttressed
from the eighteenth century onwards by legislation. An Act
passed in 1710 (9 Anne, c.5) secured that (with certain limited
exceptions) every member of the House of Commons was
liable to furnish proof that he had an income from landed
property, knights of the shire £600 and burgesses £300 per
annum. The underlying theory was that it was landed property
rather than people that merited parliamentary representation.
In 1838 personal property was made to rank with landed
property as a qualification, but in substance the reliance on
landed property continued (despite a fair amount of evidence
of manufactured or fraudulent qualifications) until abolished

1

by a measure introduced by Locke King in 1858. The result of the landed property qualification on land-holding patterns amongst knights of the shire and the peerage is indicated by Porritt in *The Unreformed House of Commons* (p. 173) when he states that "subsequent to the Act of 1710, peers with younger sons were usually careful, in the settlements to their families, to provide these sons with a sufficient income derived from land to furnish the requisite passport into the House of Commons." This in fact resulted in the burdening of the land with rent charges in their favour.

In addition to the purely legal requirement of a landed property qualification, there were other important economic and social factors which favoured the entry to parliament of the wealthier landed gentry. Election expenses, which in the nineteenth century and even earlier, might amount to sums up to £100,000 were first by usage and from 1745 onwards by law, the personal responsibility of the candidate. The fact that there were no secret ballots until 1872, nor effective laws against corruption until 1883 encouraged bribery, intimidation and a brisk trade in "forty-shilling" freeholds to pliant voters. All this demanded substantial assets on which to call. In the frequent case where an election was not contested, it was traditional to support the local squire or his nominee who, as part of the tacit understanding, would not collect the full rent from tenant farmers in a bad year. Even more important in terms of everyday life was the landowner's position as justice of the peace. It was enacted in 1589 that justices should be the most sufficient knights, esquires and gentlemen of the land and a property qualification, land to the value of £100 a year, was required until 1906. Apart from their judicial work, virtually the whole of the administration of local government outside the boroughs was in their hands until the advent of county, parish and district councils in the nineteenth century. These are the bare historical facts—but for the "feel" of the nexus between landowning and political power the reader should explore the works of the Victorian novelists.

The conveyancing devices, particularly the strict settlement, which landowners used to keep landholdings in the family basically by a voluntary form of primogeniture (while at the same time giving interests in the land to spouses and younger children) will be explored later. We must now complete the picture by attempting some explanation of why it is now comparatively rare to find large tracts of land in England still the subject of the traditional family settlement. There are in essence two reasons, one economic and one fiscal.

The economic reason is that from about the middle of the nineteenth century onwards it became plain that there was no inherent superiority in land as an investment for wealth. Investment in land which had been in the family for many years had, it is true, a strong sentimental attraction, but at this time the growth of the joint stock company combined with readily available facilities for lending money at interest, whether privately or to the government, provided alternative uses for wealth. England was becoming more of a trading than of an agricultural nation and the demand for coal and other minerals made it more desirable for mineral leases to be granted for exploitation of the underground wealth of the land. The growth of the population also put pressure on land for housing development. Land subject to the traditional family settlements was ill-suited for these purposes. Large tracts were vested in limited owners with inadequate powers of disposition, the land itself being burdened with charges in favour of other members of the family. Agricultural depression, too, became an issue in 1879 when the government appointed a Royal Commission to investigate the condition of farmers. The depression was caused basically by the repeal of the Corn Laws which after a time resulted in the cheap importation of foreign grain. Farming tended to be inefficient and unscientific and tenant farmers suffered particularly badly. Landlords were forced to lower rents, but the fixed charges payable out of their land, if settled, remained. The result in their case too was a decline in standards of living. (In presenting the Settled Land Bill in 1882 Lord Cairns emphasised that the Bill's proposals were consistent with the evidence given to the Royal Commission mentioned above (see *Hansard*, Vol. CCLXVI, p. 1076). Consequently the problem became sufficiently acute to justify legislative intervention and there followed, accordingly, the Settled Land Acts. These Acts effectively empowered the limited owner to dispose of the land free from the interests attaching to it under the settlement (the process of "overreaching") so that it became much less easy for any settlor to ordain whether the family wealth should be held in the form of land or personalty.

The fiscal reason stems from the drastic steepening of the rates of income tax, surtax and estate duty since the early 1900s. The top marginal rates of income tax (including surtax have risen as follows : 1900—1/0d. (5p.); 1935—12/9d. (64p.); 1946—19/6d. (98p.); 1969—18/3d. (91p.). In 1972 investment incomes (*i.e.* incomes not attracting earned income relief) attracted a top marginal rate of $88\frac{3}{4}$ at approximately £15,000. The rise in estate duty rates is equally dramatic, and potentially more catastrophic for landowners. When introduced in 1894 the top rate (for estates over £1 million) was 8 per cent. This was raised to 20 per cent in 1914, 40 per cent in 1925 and so on until from 1949 to 1971 a top rate of 80 per cent has been imposed. The Finance Act 1972 lowers the top marginal rate to 75 per cent on property over £500,000 but is still more severe in real terms than the 1949 scale introduced by Sir Stafford Cripps (see *Budget Statement*, 891 H.C. Deb. 1380-1381). The impact of taxation, which bears on the nominal value of money, has been increased by a steady decline in the real value (or purchasing power) of the currency. Apart from a period between the wars, the average loss in value of the pound since 1900 has been about 4 per cent per annum. This reduces the value of £1 to 1/4d. (7p.) over seventy years. These taxes are adverse to large landholdings in that as far as taxes on income are concerned, in order to retain spending power it is necessary to keep raising rents (where not controlled by statute) or otherwise make the land yield money, and owners were often either unable or unwilling to do this. Estate duty is attracted on the death of each limited owner, not just on the actuarial value of his life interest but on the full capital value of the land aggregated, usually, with his personally-owned property. When it is realised that to sell the land to raise the duty would be quite contrary to the spirit of the traditional family settlement, the predicament which landowners found themselves in can be grasped.

The decimation of the younger members of families in the First World War led to the greatest transfer of land in English history and spelt the final demise of the family settlement. From the 1920s settlements of land were drafted not primarily to keep land in the family but to preserve wealth as far as possible from the ravages of taxation. The settlement had changed from a device which attracted taxation like a magnet, to one, if skilfully used, which helps to mitigate its effect while allowing the beneficiaries to enjoy the land for a limited time *in specie*. Its use has changed, correspondingly, from being the exclusive preserve of the landed gentry to the common property of anyone who owns a house of any substance and who wishes to mitigate the impact of duty when it passes on his death, as permitted expressly by law. This aspect of the matter is looked at in detail in Chapter 7.

CHAPTER 2

THE GENESIS AND STRUCTURE OF THE STRICT SETTLEMENT

1. The development of the life estate and estate tail

As Roger North said, "To say truth, although it is not necessary for counsel to know what the history of a point is, but to know how it stands resolved, yet it is a wonderful accomplishment, and, without it, a lawyer cannot be accounted learned in the law." In the case of settlements of land, as in most other facets of English land law, one could add that without some appreciation of the genesis of certain concepts or conveyancing devices, a full understanding of the strict settlement, and from that, of the modern position, is impossible.

(a) *The life estate*

The family settlement of land consisted basically of a combination in succession of two freehold estates, the life estate and the entail. The life estate found in early feudal times was the maximum length of a grant of land from lord to tenant—"the tenure was for life, the lord resuming the land on the death of the tenant, and granting it out anew" (Hayes, *Introduction to Conveyancing*). Later, when it became understood that a grant of land could be in fee, that is that it was capable of descending to the heirs-general of the tenant or those of his assignee, it became common to carve life estates out of these greater estates. Originally such life estates were more in the nature of leases for life, a freehold estate held subject to an economic rent. Later, reports in the Year Books for the reigns of Edward II and Edward III, encompassing most of the fourteenth century, contain examples of recognisable family settlements commencing with a limitation by the settlor of a life interest to himself (and see "Shelley's Ghost," A. D. Hargreaves, (1938) 54 L.Q.R. 70).

(b) The entail

The entail, anatomically the guts of the strict settlement, was given birth by statute, namely *De Donis Conditionalibus* (Statute of Westminster II, 1285), though "conditional fees" were known earlier and were designed to ensure descent of land to the donee's heirs of the body, with reversion to the grantor on failure of the donee's issue. *De Donis* was passed to prevent the tendency of the courts to construe such conditional fees as fees simple conditional on the birth of an heir (thus defeating the expectations of the issue and the reversion to the grantor) and to ensure instead that the land should not be capable of alienation by the donee but should pass to the grantee's descendants. In the words of the statute, "the King has ordained that the will of the donor, according to the form of the deed manifestly expressed, shall be from henceforth observed and so that they to whom the land was given upon condition shall have no power to alienate the land so given but that it shall remain unto the issue of them to whom it was given after their death or shall revert unto the donor or his heirs if issue fail. . . ."

Although, as can be seen, *De Donis* purported to be merely a conservative measure, the end result was the emergence of a new estate of freehold, the fee tail (*feodum talliatum* or "cut down fee"). Although the statute is defectively drafted in that it does not make clear whether the prohibition against alienation extends to the issue of the donee, nevertheless as developed by the judges the law effectively forbade the artificial destruction of entails, which continued as long as there were heirs of the prescribed class, until about the time of *Taltarum's Case* (1472, Y.B. 12 Edw. IV 19).

Entails were, and are, created by using the correct words of limitation which, traditionally, consist of the words "heirs" followed by words of procreation—*e.g.* "of his body." Entails can be "general," that is where the descent is not limited to the issue of a specified spouse, or "special," where the descent is so limited. The entail, whether special or general can, in addition, be subdivided into tails male, where descent must be traced exclusively through male descendants, and tails female, where, correspondingly, only female heirs may take (though this device was never employed in practice). The following chart summarises the position as to the relevant words of limitation, though as regards the "common law words" sufficient to create an entail by will it should be noted that considerably greater latitude was allowed until 1926.

Type of entail	Common law words (deeds)	Statutory alternative under Conveyancing Act 1881 and Law of Property Act 1925
Tails General	To X and the heirs of his body	To X in tail.
	To X and the heirs male of his body	To X in tail male.
Special Tail	To X and the heirs [male] begotten on the body of his wife Y.	(None)

In the case of a special tail, it will be seen that if the specified spouse dies without issue the curtailed interest in question is bound to determine on the tenant in tail's death. Such tenant in tail is termed "a tenant in tail after possibility of issue extinct" or, for short, "a tenant in tail after possibility" and he cannot bar the entail (Fines and Recoveries Act 1833, s. 18) though he may sell as limited owner under the Settled Land Act 1925 (s. 20(1)(i)).

The creation of an inalienable estate was not universally regarded as a blessing. The Crown was itself prejudiced by the fact that the estate was not forfeitable for treason or felony and purchasers and lessees were prejudiced by parting with money in return for conveyances and leases of land which transpired to be entailed and hence incapable of being alienated. Despite these defects, as Blackstone says (Vol. II, p. 116) "But as the nobility were always fond of this statute, [*De Donis*] because it preserved their family estates from forfeiture, there was little hope of procuring repeal by the legislature...."

Taltarum's Case indicates that the device of the common recovery was accepted by the courts as effective to bar entails (*i.e.* to permit the tenant in tail to alienate the entire fee simple estate in the land). The finer details of this originally collusive and eventually entirely fictitious action ceased to be of practical significance so long ago that it would be unjustifiable in detail to expound them. Suffice it to say that the tenant in tail in possession would "suffer a recovery" as a result of an action brought against him by a friend (the demandant) who claimed title to the land in fee simple. It was essential for the tenant in tail to join in a third party, alleged to be the original grantor of the entail, by "vouching him to warranty," *i.e.* demanding from him land of equal value to the entailed land to recompense for the land recovered by the demandant. Judgment was accordingly entered against the third party, a man of straw who was usually the Court Crier. The net effect was that the demandant became possessed of an estate in fee simple, of which he would then dispose according to the tenant in tail's wishes, while the issue and the remaindermen were barred without even the compensation of land of equal value. This action, as later developed, degenerated from fantasy to farce when in the course of a "recovery with double voucher" the demandant craved leave to confer in private with "the common vouchee" *i.e.* the Court Crier. The court would accordingly give leave, the parties would leave the courtroom and the common vouchee would then flee until his services were required in another case.

The fine, an alternative way of barring entails, was a much older collusive action which had been specifically prohibited as an entail-barring device in *De Donis* itself. This prohibition was removed by benevolent judicial interpretation of the Statute of Fines in 1489 and confirmation of this interpretation by statute in 1540. A fine was a compromise of a fictitious personal action, made by leave of the court, whereby the land in question was acknowledged to be the right of one of them. The judgment had the effect of a judgment in a writ of right, the highest form of real action, the judgment putting an end (*finis*) both to the action and all other disputes concerning the title to the land. In fact the fine constituted an effective conveyance of land since the final concord (that A admitted B's right to the land) was indented in a tripartite indenture, the bottom copy of which, known as the foot, formed part of the record of the King's Courts, and ensured full recognition therein. (It has been suggested that the ritual significance of the part of the court in this stems from the confusion between legislation and litigation, the court being the source of law and justice.)

Of the two collusive actions, a common recovery had the advantage that it produced a fee simple absolute. A fine, on the other hand, produced a lesser estate, namely a base fee. A base fee of the variety relevant here is fee simple determinable upon failure of the heirs of the body of the grantor. A fine successfully levied would bar the issue of the tenant in tail but not the ultimate remainderman or reversioner. Against this, a common recovery, being a real action, could only be brought against or with the co-operation of the person *seised* of the land. This posed no problems if the tenant in tail was seised of the land, but if his estate were preceded by a subsisting prior estate—*e.g.* a life estate, the life tenant's concurrence was essential. A fine was in essence a personal action and could be brought by a person desiring to bar his own issue without the consent of the person seised.

The fine and the recovery became part of the fabric of English law. Hamlet, in the graveyard scene (Act V, sc. 1) remarks *vis à vis* a skull, "This fellow might be in's time a great buyer of land, with his statutes, his recognizances, his fines, his double vouchers, his recoveries: is this the fine of his fines, and the recovery of his recoveries, to have his fine pate full of fine dirt? Will his vouchers vouch him no more of his purchases, and double ones too, than the length and breadth of a pair of indentures?" In the nineteenth century a more critical approach to the law and the administration of justice becomes apparent and these proceedings, which had become purely formal, were criticised by the Attorney-General in 1833 as "involving enormous and unnecessary expense, and necessitating the conduct of proceedings through no less than twenty offices, in each of which danger, delay and expense had to be faced." As a result of recommendations made by the Real Property Commissioners in 1829 a major change in the law was introduced by the Fines and Recoveries Act 1833 which abolished fines and recoveries and substituted a much simpler device for barring entails. (Even this sensible measure was apparently opposed, on the ground that "it would render useless the 'lean and wasteful learning' which was then stored away in the brains of Conveyancing Counsel" —see Sir A. Underhill in *A Century of Law Reform*).

The 1833 Act, most of which still remains on the statute book, was a measure of estimable clarity and section 15 states ". . . every actual tenant in tail, whether in possession, remainder, contingency or otherwise, shall have full power to dispose of for an estate in fee simple absolute or for any less estate the lands entailed, as against all persons claiming the lands entailed by force of any estate tail . . . and also as against all persons . . . whose estates are to take effect after the determination or in defeasance of any such estate tail." The deed by which the entail is barred is termed a "disentailing assurance." The process is straightforward if the barring is effected by the tenant in tail *in possession*. He simply executes the assurance in favour of a trustee for himself if he wishes to enlarge the entail into a fee simple, or if he wishes to alienate the fee simple the disentailing assurance is made in favour of the grantee. The Law of Property Act 1925 (s. 133) abolished the requirement that the deed should be enrolled.

If the tenant in tail is in remainder rather than in possession, the Act ingeniously constructs a system under which the tenant is in much the same position as he would have been before the Act was passed. It will be remembered that in order to be effective, the common recovery must have been brought with the concurrence of the freehold tenant seised of the land. The Act (s. 22) therefore stipulates that "... if, at the time when there shall be a tenant in tail of lands under a settlement, there shall be subsisting in the same lands or any of them, under the same settlement, any estate ... prior to the estate tail, then the person who shall be the owner of the prior estate, or the first of such prior estates if more than one then subsisting under the same settlement ... shall be the protector of the settlement...." The significance of this provision is that it preserves the previous position under which a remainderman in tail could only create a base fee in remainder (*i.e.* by levying a fine) unless the collaboration of the person seised of a freehold estate was obtained. Thus, for example, if land is limited to X for life, with remainder to Y in tail, remainder to Z in fee simple, X is the protector of the settlement and in order that Y can disentail so as to enlarge his interest into a fee simple, he must obtain the consent of X either (and in practice) in the disentailing assurance itself or in an earlier or contemporaneous deed (ss. 34, 42). If he does so the result will be that Y holds the fee simple absolute subject only to X's life interest, which is implicitly preserved (s. 15, *ante*). If for some reason X's consent is not obtained, the tenant in tail may still dispose of the land but the effect will be to produce a base fee as opposed to a fee simple absolute (s. 34). Thus, if in the above example Y disentails without X's consent, X's issue are barred but Z's estate in remainder continues to subsist and will vest in possession on failure of Y's issue. It was held in *Re Blandy Jenkins' Estate* [1917] 1 Ch. 46 that to qualify as protector the owner of the prior estate must be a *beneficial* owner. This decision was reluctantly followed in *Re Darnley's Will Trusts* [1970] 1 W.L.R. 405, where the prior estate in question was one held on discretionary trusts during a stipulated life time. Pennycuick J. pointed out that the earlier case seemed to have been decided without regard to section 33 of the 1833 Act which he interpreted as appointing the court the protector in these circumstances.

(c) Life and entailed interests after 1925

(i) *Life interests.* As a result of the policy of the Law of Property Act 1925 (s. 1) of reducing the number of legal estates capable of existing in land to two, interests in land for life can exist as equitable interests only in England. In Ireland and those parts of the Commonwealth which have adopted unreformed English land law the life estate continues as a legal estate of freehold.

(ii) *Entails.* By the same token, in England the former fee tail can now only exist as an entailed interest. In addition the Law of Property Act 1925 permitted the creation of entailed interests "by way of trust in any property, real or personal"— *i.e.* entails can now subsist in personalty. Entails and base fees in possession may also be barred by will (provided there is a specific reference to the entailed property therein) (s. 176) and disentailing assurances need not be enrolled (s. 133).

(iii) *Problems concerning the barring of entails after 1925.* Thus stated, the position appears to be fairly simple. Since an entail must be equitable, there must be a trust (since the legal estate in fee simple is separate from the equitable interest). Nevertheless the old procedure for barring entails under the Fines and Recoveries Act 1833 continues to apply *mutatis mutandis*, the Ninth Schedule of the Law of Property (Amendment) Act 1924 merely stating that the 1833 Act "remains in force in regard to dealings with entailed interests as equitable interests."

Unfortunately the interaction of the above provisions with the scheme imposed on (*inter alia*) entailed land by the Settled Land Act 1925 is far from simple, and is, surprisingly, hardly touched upon by the standard textbooks. An examination of the procedure for the alienation of entailed land is, however, a valuable exercise in comprehending the working of the law in this area. As will be seen, a tenant in tail whose interest is in possession is by section 20 of the Settled Land Act 1925 given all the powers of a tenant for life under that Act. In addition, by section 4 read with section 20(2), the vesting deed will vest in such tenant in tail the whole legal estate the subject of the settlement. The question then arises as to precisely what happens if the tenant in tail wishes to disentail. It is clear that the disentailing assurance will operate in equity only, so that the tenant in tail by disentailing will vest in himself (normally) ("normally" because after 1925 leaseholds may be entailed) the equitable fee simple.

Let us suppose, by way of a simple example, that under the will of Lord Fauntleroy Blackacre is devised "to John Smith in tail with remainder to Albert Jenkins in fee simple." The will was proved in the Principal Probate Registry on December 5, 1960, and appoints X and Y executors and trustees for the purposes of the Settled Land Act 1925. A little later X and Y execute a vesting instrument under which the whole legal estate in Blackacre is vested in John Smith as tenant in tail having the powers and position of a tenant for life under the Settled Land Act 1925. John Smith now wishes to bar the entailed interest, and may do so by a disentailing assurance of which the following is an example:

THIS DEED OF DISENTAIL made the 5th day of January 1971 BETWEEN JOHN SMITH [etc.] (hereinafter called "Mr. Smith") of the one part and X of [etc.] and Y of [etc.] (hereinafter called "the Trustees") of the other part WITNESSETH that Mr. Smith hereby conveys unto the Trustees ALL the freehold land and property more particularly mentioned in the Schedule hereto and comprised in a Vesting Assent dated [etc.] and made [etc.] and of which Mr. Smith is now tenant in tail in possession in equity under the Will of Lord Fauntleroy dated [etc.] and proved in the Principal Probate Registry on the 5th day of December 1960 To hold the same unto the Trustees in fee simple freed and discharged from all interests in tail of Mr. Smith and from all estates interests rights and

powers to take effect after the determination or in defeasance
of any such interests in tail IN TRUST for Mr. Smith for an
equitable estate in fee simple
IN WITNESS etc.

THE SCHEDULE above referred to
[Particulars of Blackacre]

(Executed by all parties and attested).

The following points should be noted in relation to the
above example:

(1) Section 40 of the 1833 Act specifically stipulates that
the assurance should be by deed, and this stipulation continues
to apply even though the instrument is a conveyance of an
equitable interest.

(2) As the 1833 Act envisages a "disposition" of land the
pre-1926 practice was for the tenant in tail to convey to the
grantees to uses who held either in trust for the tenant in
tail or to such uses as he should appoint. The old practice
has here been followed and the trustees of the settlement
have been chosen for the purpose, though there would appear
to be no objection to the tenant in tail conveying to himself
—see Law of Property Act 1925 (s. 72(3) and Sched. 6,
Specimen No. 1). The position if the land were conveyed
direct to a purchaser is discussed below.

(3) The result of the habendum is that the trustees are
trustees of an equitable interest. They hold as bare trustees for
Mr. Smith and the equitable "estate" which vests in them
would merge in that of Mr. Smith.

(4) The trustees should execute the deed to prevent any
possibility of a future disclaimer by them, as occurred in
Peacock v. *Eastland* ((1870) L.R. 10 Eq. 17). There the
trustees who had not executed the deed disclaimed the trusts
and the disentailing assurance was held void.

Having, then, vested the entire equitable fee simple in Mr.
Smith it is now necessary to consider what would have to be
done if Mr. Smith later desired to sell the entire legal estate
in Blackacre. It will be recalled that as far as the outside
world is concerned the settlement is still on foot and the

trustees for the purposes of the Settled Land Act 1925 remain undischarged. Section 18(1) would thus make any purported disposition (other than as authorised by the Act) of the legal estate by Mr. Smith (the "tenant for life") void. The only course open to Mr. Smith would be, then, to call for a deed of discharge under section 17 of the Settled Land Act 1925 by which the trustees would declare that they are discharged from the trusts. Mr. Smith could then deal with the legal estate freely.

If, at the time of the disentailing transaction, Mr. Smith had the intention of selling Blackacre, two alternative courses would be available. Firstly he could disentail by disposing of the land direct to a purchaser in fee simple, (a course mentioned in *Megarry and Wade* (at p. 93)). This would extend only to the equitable fee simple, but by section 42(4)(ii) of the Law of Property Act 1925, the contract for the sale of Blackacre would be deemed to extend to the legal estate therein (because the vendor had "power to vest such legal estate in himself"). But as the settlement is still *notionally* subsisting the legal estate therein remains vested in Mr. Smith, so unless he obtains a deed of discharge as before and then conveys to the purchaser, a conveyance by Mr. Smith as tenant for life would be necessary. This solution is neither satisfactory nor sensible and serves only to demonstrate the needless complexity of the modern law. The better alternative would be for Mr. Smith to convey the legal estate, as tenant for life, to the purchaser and then disentail the purchase money.

However cumbersome the process of barring entails may be, the estate duty consequences of not doing so and allowing the entailed land to pass on the tenant in tail's death can be disastrous, as is explained later in this book. Indeed a legal adviser who fails to inform a tenant in tail that his interest can be barred may be guilty of negligence—see *Otter* v. *Church, Adams, Tatham & Co.* ([1953] 1 W.L.R. 156). However, recent cases suggest that it may not always be clear who had the right to bar an entail within the Fines and Recoveries Act 1833, s. 15 (considered above, p. 11). In

Re St. Albans' Will Trust ([1963] Ch. 365) the 10th Duke of St. Albans had by will dated December 18, 1896 given certain estates to the use of every successive son of his own for life, with remainder to the sons of that son in tail male "and on failure of such issue to the use of the person who on my death or the failure of my male issue (which shall last happen) shall become Duke of St. Albans in tail male." The 12th Duke was 87 years old and had no issue. If he died without issue C.B. would become Duke. It was held that C.B.'s disentail with the consent of the 12th Duke as protector was effective to bar the entail if the contingency took place, until when C.B. had a "corresponding contingent interest in remainder" (*per* Pennycuick J. at p. 371).

The reasoning in this case was, however, doubted and the decision (in so far as it depended on C.B. having a *contingent* interest) not followed in *Re Earl of Middleton's Will Trusts* ([1969] 1 Ch. 600). In the opinion of Stamp J. the interest of C.B. in the *St. Albans'* case was a mere *spes successionis*, as opposed to a contingent interest, and it is by no means certain that a person with a mere *spes* can bar the entail to which he hopes to succeed (see argument of counsel, R. E. Megarry, in the *St. Albans'* case at pp. 368-369). The point was illustrated by Stamp J. thus (at p. 607): "A gift to A, if on the death of B he shall be heir of B ... confers on A a present interest called contingent and which becomes vested if, on the death of B, A has the required characteristic. On the other hand, a gift to whomsoever shall at the death of B, a living person, be the heir of B ... in my judgment confers no interest upon anyone until the death of B, when you inquire who has the required characteristic."

(*iv*) *The problem of descent.* A further, and quite different problem, may arise in deciding to whom the entailed interest descends on the death of a tenant who has not barred it in his life time or by will. Here, the old rules of descent applicable before 1926 as section 130(4) of the Law of Property Act 1925 makes clear:

"In default of and subject to the execution of a disentailing assurance or the exercise of the testamentary power conferred by this Act, an entailed interest (to the extent of the property affected) shall devolve as an equitable interest, from time to time, upon the persons who would have been successively entitled thereto as the heirs of the body (either generally or of a particular class) of the tenant in tail or other person, or as tenant by the curtesy, if the entailed interest had, before the commencement of this Act, been limited in respect of freehold land governed by the general law in force immediately before such commencement, and such law had remained unaffected."

The old rules of descent as established by common law (but altered slightly in a way not affecting entails by statute) are complex and their detail is outside the scope of this book. In essence these rules involve (a) tracing descent from the last purchaser, a "purchaser" meaning any person taking by act of parties rather than by operation of law, and in the context of entails, the donee in tail, (b) preferring male issue to female issue, the latter taking, if of equal degree, as co-parceners, (c) preferring the elder male to the younger and (d) applying the principle of representation, so that lineal descendants represent their ancestor. Thus, suppose that land is settled on X for life with remainder to his son A and the heirs of his body. At the death of A it is ascertained that he had two sons, (1) B who predeceased him leaving a son C, and (2) a younger living son D. Here A's grandson C will take the entail. If C then dies leaving two daughters only, they will inherit as co-parceners. A further application of the old canons of descent occurs where a married woman dies without having disposed of an entailed interest. Here, if issue of the marriage capable of inheriting have been born alive, and the woman's entail was not held in joint tenancy, the widower will still take a life interest in the entailed land.

These antiquated rules only apply to the descent by operation of law to realty in one other case, namely where a person was lunatic of full age before 1926 and dies intestate without recovering testamentary capacity (Administration of Estates Act 1925, s. 51(2)), a combination of circumstances which must be increasingly rare. Their preservation with respect to the descent of entailed interests was a necessary condition to the continuance of the entail as a proprietary interest in the 1925 legislation and now provides a further reason, if one were needed, for the abolition of the interest in the modern era.

2. Definitions

It is as well, before embarking on an analysis of the strict settlement to establish clearly what is meant by the term "settlement." Cheshire (pp. 140-141) states that "the word *settlement* properly so called connotes succession. Its normal meaning is any instrument or series of instruments by which successive interests are carved out of realty or personalty and under which, in the case of land, there will be at any given time some person entitled in possession to a beneficial interest for life." Megarry and Wade (at p. 287) state that "the word 'settlement' is used in a general sense for all kinds of arrangements whereby property is given to particular persons in succession." The intrinsic ambiguity in the above definitions is accentuated by Meggary and Wade when they state (at p. 296) that "the term 'settlement' in the [1882] Act meant the document itself rather than the state of affairs produced by it." It is clearly legitimate to refer to an instrument containing certain trusts as a "settlement"; indeed, the instrument itself may well so describe itself. But the danger of this usage becomes apparent when reference to "trustees of the settlement" is taken to mean, literally, trustees of the piece of paper containing the trusts when what is really intended is a reference to trustees of the *trust property* as defined in the instrument. Unfortunately this vital distinction is blurred by the legislation itself, as a comparison of section 1 of the Settled Land Act 1925 (any deed etc. containing the appropriate limitations "*creates* or is ... a settlement") with section 30 thereof (trustees of the settlement are, for example, "the persons if any, for the time being, who are *by the settlement declared to be trustees thereof* for the purposes of ... this Act") will show. The same point was made by Romer J. in *Re Ogle's Settled Estates* ([1927] 1 Ch. 229) in these words: "In some parts of the Act no doubt 'settlement' means merely the document or documents creating the settlement: see, for example, sections 1(4), 47 and 64. But in general a settlement, for the purposes of the Act, is a state of affairs in relation to certain land, brought about, or deemed to have been brought about by one or more documents the particular state of affairs being one or more of those specified in subsections (*i*) to (*v*) of section 1(1)."

In modern English law a further distinction must be made between "settlements" and "trusts for sale." Although both terms denote arrangements whereby property is carved up into successive limited interests, the term "settlement" as applied to land is often used to refer to settlements other than by way of trust for sale. This is no doubt because such settlements are governed by the Settled Land Act 1925 whereas land subject to an "immediate binding trust for sale" is expressly excluded from the Settled Land Act 1925 (s. 1(7)) and is governed instead by the Law of Property Act 1925. In so far as successive interests are created under a trust for sale, it is nevertheless entirely appropriate to refer to the arrangement as a "settlement by way of trust for sale."

3. Outline of the strict settlement

The sixteenth century saw the rise of a landed gentry class who, if the volume of litigation concerning land settlements is any indication, were bent on ensuring that their land was as far as possible kept in the family permanently. The evolution of the power of appointment and the legal executory interest (the Statute of Uses 1535 enabling a *legal* estate to be appointed by the former and a wide variety of *legal* future interests to be created by the latter) greatly contributed to the armoury at hand for the enterprising draftsman. But it was not until towards the end of the seventeenth century that

the model conveyances produced by a few eminent conveyancers (particularly Sir Orlando Bridgman, who "betook
himself to conveyancing at the time of the Civil Wars") produced a form of settlement satisfactory to the landowners.
The strict settlement was also upheld by the courts, who, as
a matter of policy, were very much influenced by conveyancing practice. As Lord Hardwicke remarks in *Basset* v. *Basset*
((1744) 3 Atk. 203, 208), "The uniform opinion and practice
of eminent conveyancers has always had great regard paid
to it in all courts of justice."

As already pointed out, the heart of the strict settlement
was a life interest succeeded by an entail. The rule in *Whitby*
v. *Mitchell* ((1890) 44 Ch.D. 85) in the course of its evolution
starting in the sixteenth century (see *Chudleigh's Case* (1595)
1 Co. Rep. 113b, 138) forbade the circumvention of the rule
that unbarrable entails could not be created (other than by
statute) by outlawing such devices as a limitation consisting of
innumerable successive life interests. An entail following on a
life estate was the best that could be done without violating
the perpetuity rules. However, what could not be preordained
by the settlor was nevertheless normally achieved in practice
by the device of the resettlement. This can be best explained by
an example. Suppose land stood limited to X for life with
reminder to X's first and every other son successively in tail,
the settlement dating perhaps from X's marriage. Then
suppose that X's eldest son is about to attain his majority.
On becoming of age X's son could partially bar the entail by
conveying a base fee to a purchaser or, with the consent of
his father as protector, bar it completely. Either course
would normally be regarded as against the settlor's wishes
and the family's interest. Instead, therefore, the father and
son would normally come to an arrangement whereby the property would be *resettled* for a further generation, the
eldest son obtaining in return an immediate income from the
land by way of rentcharge. The resettlement was effected by
the son, with the father's consent, disentailing so that at that
point of time the father's life interest and the son's entail
were destroyed and the land was free of the fetters of the

original settlement except as to any interests in favour of relatives (*e.g.* jointure and portions—described later) preceding the entail. The father and son would have been given, under the terms of the disentailing assurance, joint powers of appointment over the land and would resettle it by giving:

(a) a yearly rentcharge of a stipulated sum to X's eldest son during his father's lifetime (thus giving the son an income charged on the land), and subject thereto,

(b) a life interest to the father, X, which would normally be expressed to be in restoration of his former life interest, and subject thereto,

(c) a life interest to the son, and subject thereto,

(d) entailed interests to the son's sons.

(In practice there would also be jointures and portions (see below) in favour of other relatives and various "fail-safe" limitations to guard against, for example, the contingency of X's eldest son dying without issue.)

It will be seen that the fundamental principle behind the strict settlement was that no tenant in tail should ever be allowed to become entitled in possession (as opposed to in remainder). A tenant in tail in possession had unfettered power of disposition—he could break the entail by suffering a common recovery. A tenant in tail in remainder could at the most create a base fee, an interest of no great pecuniary value and a mere life tenant could create a mere interest *pur autre vie*. The finer points relating to the creation of such settlements such as the device used to prevent the premature destruction of the contingent remainders, namely the initial limitation to trustees to preserve the contingent remainders in favour of the unborn sons of the life tenant, or the creation of the settlement by employing the conveyancing device of the lease and release, are of little relevance nowadays. Nevertheless strict settlements still appear on titles which have to be investigated by solicitors—many a modern building estate stands snugly on land formerly owned by one landed family for many decades before its eventual sale for development. For this reason it is still a useful exercise to have a look at an abbreviated form of the nineteenth century strict settlement and analyse its main provisions. The following is based on the Conveyancing and Law of Property Act, ("the Conveyancing Act 1881"), Fourth Schedule, and represents the settlement of land owned by the intended husband in contemplation of his forthcoming marriage. Valuable consideration is deemed to have been given by the future spouse and unborn issue (see *Macdonald* v. *Scott* [1893] A.C. 642, 650).

THIS INDENTURE made the   day of   1883 between John M. of [etc.] of the first part Jane S. of [etc.] of the second part and X of [etc.] and Y of [etc.] of the third part WITNESSETH that in consideration of the intended marriage between John M. and Jane S. John M. as settlor[1] hereby conveys to X and Y[2] all that [etc.] To hold to X and Y in fee simple to the use of John M. in fee simple until the marriage[3] and after the marriage to the use of John M. during his life without impeachment of waste[4] with remainder after his death to the use that Jane S. if she survives him may receive during the rest of her life a yearly jointure rentcharge[5] of £   to commence from his death and to be paid by equal half-yearly payments the first thereof to be made at the end of six calendar months from his death if she is then living or if not a proportional part to be paid at her death and subject to the before-mentioned rentcharge to the use of X and Y for a term of 500 years without impeachment of waste on the trusts herein-after declared[6] and subject thereto to the use of the first and other sons of John M. and Jane S. successively according to seniority in tail male with remainder [insert here, if thought desirable, to the use of the same first and other sons successively according to seniority in tail with remainder] to the use of all the daughters of John M. and Jane S. in equal shares as tenants in common in tail with cross remainders between them in tail with remainder to the use of John M. in fee simple.[7] [Insert trusts of term of 500 years for raising portions; also, if required, power to charge jointure and portions on a future marriage; also

powers of sale, exchange, and partition, and other powers
and provisions, if and as desired].

IN WITNESS, etc.

Explanatory notes

(1) A conveyance "as settlor" merely imports a covenant by
the husband for further assurance—*i.e.* that he will do anything necessary to perfect the trustee's title to the land should
this conveyance be defective (see Conveyancing Act 1881,
s. 7(1)(*e*) and Law of Property Act 1925, s. 76(1)(*e*)).

(2) X and Y are the trustees and it would be made clear
that they were trustees for the purposes of the Settled Land
Act 1882.

(3) This is a shifting use—*i.e.* John's legal fee simple (the
use being executed) is cut short on his marriage.

(4) Unless made "unimpeachable of waste" John as a life
tenant would be liable for voluntary waste. As he has been
made unimpeachable, he may, for instance, open and work
mines or cut timber.

(5) A "jointure" in this context is an annual payment during
widowhood secured on the land by a legal rentcharge. A
rentchargee has stringent remedies against the land to enforce
payment—see Conveyancing Act 1881, s. 44 and Law of
Property Act 1925, s. 121. This particular settlement does
not include "pin money" for Jane during John's life. Had it
done so its first limitation would have been to the use that
the wife may receive, during the joint lives of the spouses, a
small annual amount secured by a rentcharge on the land.
As its name indicates, this payment would have been intended
to meet the wife's personal expenses.

(6) The trusts referred to here are those relating to the
raising of "portions." Portions are lump sums of capital provided for the younger children on attaining majority, as compensation for not taking interests in the land. It will be noted
that the limitation is "to hold to X and Y in fee simple ...
to the use of X and Y for a term of 500 years. ..." The trustees
would therefore take a *legal* term of 500 years under the

Statute of Uses without the necessity of entry on the land, and also without payment of rent. Furthermore, as the portions terms precede the estates tail, they cannot be defeated by the tenant in tail barring the fee tail. The term could, under the usual trusts, be assigned or mortgaged by the trustees to raise the portions if necessary, though in practice the tenant for life in order to disencumber the estate often payed the portions out of his own pocket. When the portions were paid the term of 500 years would become a "satisfied term" and cease (Satisfied Terms Act 1845 and Law of Property Act 1925, s. 5).

(7) These are the interests in remainder and take effect here as legal contingent remainders. The effect here is, briefly, that the eldest son and his successive *male* heirs would take. If the eldest son's male issue failed the other sons *of the parties to the marriage* would take in order of seniority in tail male. If at any stage all the male issue fails, the process is repeated from the start so that under the tail general which supersedes the tail male, female issue would be likely to benefit. The effect of the cross-remainders to the daughters can be illustrated by supposing John and Jane had only two children, both daughters. They would take one undivided half share each in tail. If one of those daughters died without issue the survivor would take her deceased sister's share. There is an ultimate remainder to the settlor in fee simple which would become operative, for example, on the settlor's dying childless.

4. Modern marriage settlements

Modern settlements are discussed later and the impact of modern taxation on their form is examined (see Chapter 7) but at this stage it is perhaps useful to point out that the modern equivalent of the above would, or where the form is not affected by statute would be likely to, contain the following major variations:

(1) Assuming the settlement was drafted to take effect under the Settled Land Act 1925, the trust instrument would

not include a conveyance of the property. This would be contained in a separate vesting deed either in favour of the tenant for life, or if framed as a discretionary settlement, to the trustees as statutory owner. (Examples of a vesting deed and trust instrument of a marriage settlement containing the traditional (and virtually obsolete) trusts are contained in Forms 2 and 3 of the First Schedule of the Settled Land Act 1925.)

(2) As regards the beneficial interests to be given to the children, entails would probably not be created. The husband or the wife, or both successively, are likely to be given a power to appoint the property by deed or will to one or more of the children or remoter issue of the intended marriage for such estates or interests as were stipulated on exercising the power.

CHAPTER 3

THE GENESIS OF THE MODERN LEGISLATION

1. Introduction

It was pointed out in Chapter 1 that because of the economic changes affecting the country in the nineteenth century together with the growth in population, the existence of large tracts of land "in fetters" became a serious problem. The basic difficulties were:

(a) The traditional settlement and resettlement by intention resulted in the tenant in possession having, at the most, a life estate. Under the general law he could not dispose of more than was vested beneficially in him or grant leases binding upon his successors;

(b) Efficient management of the land was inhibited by the lack of any facility of drawing on capital to effect improvements or rebuilding. Exploitation of mineral wealth under the land was prevented by the law of waste unless the tenant was expressly unimpeachable of waste;

(c) The interests of other members of the family under the settlement tended to produce heavily incumbered estates, e.g. by virtue of the rentcharges secured on the land to raise jointures or the mortgages which had been effected to raise the capital sums needed for portions.

Whilst these problems were serious, it would distort the true position to fail to mention that well-drawn settlements managed to mitigate the position by ingenious conveyancing. By vesting the land in feoffees to such uses as may be appointed and giving either the tenant for life or some other person the power to appoint the settled property, the land could effectively be conveyed to a purchaser and the beneficial

27

interests overreached. It was also usual to give to the tenant for life power to grant agricultural leases of up to twenty-one years and building leases of up to ninety years. Nevertheless, in the case of a will made without proper legal advice such powers would probably be omitted entirely and in other cases draftsmen tended to err on the side of caution and confer insufficient or restrictive powers. Where the family found itself burdened with a rigid settlement the only way to remedy the situation was to obtain a private Act of Parliament. A glance at the private Acts passed in 1840 gives a good indication of the problem (and also suggests that it was only the rich who could afford the luxury of this process). Here are a few random examples:

Cap. 8   An Act to enable the Trustees of the Will of the late Roger Forrest the elder to make Grants in Fee, and Leases for years at Reserved Rents, of certain parts of his Trust Estates, situate in the Parish of Blackburn in the County of Lancaster.

Cap. 20   An Act for extending the Powers of Sale and Exchange contained in the Will of George Isaac Mowbray Esquire, deceased, and for other purposes.

Cap. 22   An Act to authorize the Sale of a Mansion House purchased under the Trusts of the Will of the late John Julius Angerstein Esquire, deceased, and to authorize Leases to be made of the same, and also of certain Lands devised by the said Will.

Cap. 35   An Act to enable the Trustees of the Will of the late Duke of Bridgewater to make Conveyances in Fee or Demises for long Terms of years of Parts of his Trust Estates in the Counties of Lancaster and Chester, for building on and improving the same; and to grant Leases of Coal and other Mines, and of Waste Lands.

2. Early reforms

These problems required a legislative solution. Fortunately

from the second quarter of the nineteenth century onwards the climate was ripe for reform, not only because after 1832 the influence in parliament of the landowning classes diminished but, as Simpson in his *Introduction to the History of Land Law* points out (at p. 253) "a number of able and influential lawyers allied themselves to the movement for reform; these men had the immense advantage of attacking the abuses of the system from within, and of having the technical competence to suggest and draw up concrete proposals for reform, instead of merely inveighing against this or that absurdity." Among these reformers Lord Campbell, Lord Brougham, Lord Westbury, Lord Cairns, Joshua Williams and E. P. Wolstenholme were pre-eminent. The most important of the legislation relating to land during the nineteenth century was perhaps the laying of the foundation of a system for registration of title, notably in Lord Westbury's Land Registry Act of 1862 and the superseding Land Transfer Act 1875 sponsored by Lord Cairns. The legislation relating to conveyancing generally made important reforms of a detailed character without dealing with many basic faults. Only the legislation relating to settled land possessed something of a revolutionary character, not only because its policy was to secure full alienability of settled land contrary to the settlor's implied intentions but because in prohibiting any "contracting out" of the legislation's main provisions it went contrary to the prevailing idea of *laissez-faire*.

The process started modestly with Drainage Acts, the Act of 1840 sufficiently explaining the problem in the following preamble: "Whereas much of the land in England and Ireland would be rendered permanently more productive by improved Draining, and nevertheless by reason of the great Expence thereof, Proprietors having a limited interest in such land are often unable to execute such draining. . . ." The tenant for life was accordingly empowered, with the court's consent, to raise mortgages charged on the settled estate to raise money for drainage purposes. Other Acts in the 1860s and 1870s empowered the tenant for life to effect various improvements including the erection of mansion houses and buildings of waterworks. In Ireland the acute problem of the agrarian situation prompted the passing of more radical legislation in the Incumbered Estates Acts of 1848 and 1849 and the Landed Estates Court (Ireland) Act 1858. These statutes empowered owners of settled estates to sell them through the Incumbered Estates Court, distributing the proceeds amongst incumbrancers, creditors and the former owners. The purchaser was given an absolute title by means of an instrument executed by the court. Up to 1870 some 10,655 incumbered estates had been sold pursuant to these statutes, though the economic effect of such large scale land-dumping was found to be far from beneficial.

A parallel development of greater importance was the passing of the Settled Estates Act 1856, subsequently replaced by the Settled Estates Act 1877. The basis of this legislation was that dealings in settled land could be authorised by the court as a substitute for a private Act of Parliament. The Chancery Division of the High Court could authorise sales, exchanges and partitions. Leases could also be sanctioned for 21 years (35 years in Ireland) for agricultural or occupational purposes, 40 years for mining, 60 years for repairing leases and 99 years for building purposes (s. 4); for periods of up to 21 years (35 years in Ireland) the tenant for life could make leases without the court's sanction, though the settlor could negative this. Indeed the underlying weakness of the Act was that the settlor could, in effect, contract out of the Act altogether (s. 38). In addition, before sanctioning any transaction the court would normally be obliged to obtain consents of beneficiaries, though these could be dispensed with (ss. 26-29). The end result was a circumscribed order which by trying to please all the beneficiaries tended to please no one. The Act was, out of abundance of caution, never repealed on the passing of the Settled Lands Acts 1882-1890 (and still remains on the statute book in Ireland) though its provisions are almost entirely otiose.

3. The Settled Land Act 1882

The Settled Land Act 1882 was quite a different matter and remains the basis of modern English law in so far as it was substantially reincarnated in the 1925 Act. The 1882 Act was drafted by E. P. Wolstenholme. Creative draftsmen are not prone to attract much notice amongst the public or academic writers, yet the claim to fame of some of their number is in many ways quite as great as that of outstanding members of the judiciary. If this sounds startling, the reader should consider the extraordinarily complex conceptual problems which arise when devising and implementing a fool-proof scheme to solve or mitigate the many and pressing problems of mid-nineteenth century conveyancing. Unlike the judiciary, the draftsman's task is not limited to solving one particular problem after it has arisen. He must first visualise a scheme in its totality and then, when drafting it, cater for every foreseeable contingency, every fringe eventuality, that may arise. The resulting detailed legislation must then be clear in fundamental principle without being inadequate to meet detailed problems of implementation. E. P. Wolstenholme (1824-1908) a conveyancing counsel of the court for some twenty-eight years, was a draftsman of genius. He is described as having been "a man of indefatigable industry, a master in the art of terse and lucid draftsmanship and, in the devising of bold and original schemes to rescue his clients from difficulties, almost without an equal." Wolstenholme also drafted the Conveyancing Act 1881 and in 1880 Lord Cairns wrote, referring to the conveyancing and settled land legislation, that "I cannot but look upon them as the most remarkable efforts in legislation since the Fines and Recoveries Act." On his death in 1908 an article in the Solicitors' Journal (52 S. J. 494) states: "It is even now scarcely appreciated with how much skill and care the schemes contained in the Bills are worked out; but the astonishing thing is that they should have been done by a man in the midst of an overwhelming practice, and that all this anxious and difficult work should have been done by Mr. Wolstenholme without fee or reward of any kind." (See Preface to Wolstenholme's *Conveyancing and Settled Land Acts,* and Foreword by Megarry J. to Wolstenholme and Cherry's *Conveyancing Statutes,* 13th ed.)

The basic purpose of the Act was to vest in the person for the time being having an interest in possession in the use or enjoyment of the land, virtually complete dominion over it. At the same time it was ensured that the corpus of the property, whether represented by realty or personalty, should be preserved for successors in title to the limited owner under the settlement. The act was amended as regards minor details in 1884, 1887, 1889 and 1890 and the legislation is together referred to as "the Settled Land Acts 1882-90."

The principle of vesting almost complete control in a limited owner is in many ways sound. The tenant for life is likely to be the person most closely connected with the land and thus best placed to judge whether it should be sold, leased, improved or otherwise dealt with. At the same time, by virtue of these statutory and inalienable powers, the scheme (in the words of Chitty L.J. in *Re Mundy and Roper's Contract* [1899] 1 Ch. 275, 288) "facilitate[s] the striking off from the land of fetters imposed by settlements."

Nevertheless, putting so much power into the hands of one limited owner creates the following ugly possibilities or difficulties which the statutory scheme must counteract:

(1) He might abuse his powers by *e.g.* selling the settled land at an undervalue to a friend;
(2) He might abscond with the purchase money;
(3) There must be clear evidence on a dealing with the land that the person purporting to exercise the powers in question is the tenant for life (or other person having the statutory powers);
(4) If the whole legal estate in the land is not vested in one person, then the tenant for life must be given power to convey it although not vested in him—and, of course, free from the interests under the settlement.

How the draftsman attempted to solve these problems is indicated in the outline of the legislation which follows.

4. Outline of the 1882 Act

(a) Settled land and tenant for life defined

Section 2 defines a settlement as the result of any document or documents "under or by virtue of which ... any estate or interest in land, stands for the time being limited to or in trust for any persons by way of succession."

The tenant for life is "the person who is for the time being, under a settlement, beneficially entitled to possession of settled land, for his life" (s. 2(5)). Also, since a succession of interests may take many forms, *e.g.* a fee simple subject to an executory limitation over on the happening of a specific event, or an entail (where the successive interests are the fee tail followed by the fee simple remainder or reversion), section 58 of the 1882 Act defines a number of limited owners who have the powers of a tenant for life "as if each of them were a tenant for life as defined in this Act." These include tenants in tail, tenants in fee simple subject to an executory limitation over or a tenant for years determinable on life.

In addition to the above the Act tackled the position of an infant holding a legal or equitable estate in land and whether absolutely or for a limited interest. Because an infant had an irrevocable right to avoid any disposition by himself of land on or within a reasonable time of attaining his majority (see *Slator* v. *Trimble* (1861) 14 Ir. C.L.R. 342 and *Edwards* v. *Carter* [1893] A.C. 360), land thus vested in an infant became virtually unmarketable. The solution adopted was to make such land settled land with the infant the tenant for life, and then make the trustees of the settlement exercise his powers on his behalf (ss. 59, 60).

(b) Position of the tenant for life

As mentioned above, the basic problem involved in giving the tenant for life unfettered powers over the land is of devising a method whereby any abuse of power can be checked. The Act conferred extensive powers on the tenant for life of selling, leasing, mortgaging, exchanging and generally dealing with the land (which powers are further discussed *post* p. 62) and in return decreed that in exercising them that he should "have regard to the interests of all parties entitled under the settlement, and shall, in relation to the exercise thereof by him, be deemed to be in the position and to have the duties and liabilities of a trustee for those parties" (s. 53, and see the similar position in S.L.A. 1925, s. 107).

The tenant for life's fiduciary position has been considered in a number of cases since the passing of the 1882 Act, and the general conclusion is that "there is nothing in the Act to restrain [the tenant for life] from selling, whether he desires to sell because he is in debt, and wishes to increase his income ... or whether he acts from worse motives, as from mere caprice or whim, or because he is desirous of doing that which he knows would be very disagreeable to those who expect to succeed him at his death." Nevertheless "if a tenant for life attempted to commit what may be called a fraud, and proposed to sell the property for something infinitely below its real value, it would be the duty of the trustees to come to the court and ask for an injunction to restrain a sale" (*per* Pearson J. in *Wheelwright* v. *Walker* (1883) 23 Ch.D. 752). Other examples of where the court restrained the attempted exercise of a tenant for life's powers are *Middlemas* v. *Stevens* ([1901] 1 Ch. 574) where the defendant was entitled to a house during widowhood and, being about to remarry, proposed to grant a lease of the house to her prospective husband so as to continue in occupation ("not a bona fide exercise of her powers as tenant for life," *per* Joyce J.) and *Re Earl Somers* ((1895) 11 T.L.R. 567) where a teetotal tenant for life was restrained from letting a public house on the terms that no intoxicating liquor be sold.

(c) *Position of the trustees*

The trustees were such persons as fell within the definition contained in section 2(8) (as amended by s. 16 of the Act of 1890) but in the normal case were those persons "who are by the settlement declared to be trustees thereof for purposes of this Act."

In most cases the trustees had virtually no control over the land since this would be vested in the tenant for life. They were given the following main functions, which were calculated to strike a happy compromise between the evils of giving them such powers as would prejudice the tenant for life's autonomy and giving them such insignificant powers that there would be no "fail-safe" device which could operate in the last resort to restrain an irresponsible tenant for life.

(a) Notice of intended transactions of sale, exchange, partition, leasing and mortgaging had to be given to them by the tenant for life by posting a registered letter containing the notice at least one month before the transaction (with a like notice to their solicitor if known (s. 45)). This notice "may be of a general intention in that behalf" though the trustees could request further particulars (Act of 1884, s. 5) and was unnecessary before granting leases not exceeding twenty-one years at the best rent reasonably obtainable (Act of 1890, s. 7). (These provisions as to notices are reproduced almost identically in section 101 of the Settled Land Act 1925.) The object of the giving of notices is to give the trustees the opportunity of applying to the court for an injunction to restrain an improper transaction, but the 1882 Act states expressly that there is no liability "for not making, bringing, taking, or doing any such application, action, proceeding, or thing, as they might make, bring, take, or do"; (s. 42, and *cf.* S.L.A. 1925, s. 97).

(b) Dealings with the "principal mansion house" on the settled land required the *consent* of the trustees. The "principal mansion house" was defined so as to exclude farmhouses or estates not exceeding twenty-five acres (Act of 1890, s. 10).

(c) On a dealing involving capital money, that money had to be paid to the trustees or into court so that it could then either be invested by the trustees or by the court "according to the direction of the tenant for life" (s. 22). The necessity of normally paying the purchase money to the trustees met the problem of the danger of a dishonest tenant for life absconding with the proceedings of a sale which he had arranged.

(d) Proof of title

Clearly the correct identification of the tenant for life (or other person having his powers) was essential from the purchaser's point of view. A tenant for life selling under the statutory power given to him to do so by virtue of the Settled Land Acts 1882-90 would have had to satisfy his purchaser of the following:

(1) That there was a settlement within the meaning of the Acts, and the land that he proposed to buy was subject to the settlement;

(2) That the original settlor had a good title to the land settled (unless, in practice, the settlement was of long standing);

(3) That the vendor was entitled in possession under the settlement and was the person entitled to exercise the statutory powers;

(4) That the persons joined in the conveyance as recipients of the purchase money are the duly constituted trustees.

This was the one area of the overall scheme which had not been thought out thoroughly by the draftsman of the 1882 Act. Investigation of title before 1926 was in any event usually a major operation demanding as of course a far higher standard of knowledge of the theory of land law on the part of the investigating solicitor than is normally demanded nowadays. It may be that the draftsman did not regard the problems of investigating title to land held in settlement as being necessarily more acute than any other transaction. However, since the 1882 Act contained no devices for facilitating investigation of title, the result was that in order to satisfy himself on the above points the purchaser's solicitor had to make a careful perusal of documents comprising the settlement (which was often a "compound" settlement by virtue of, for example, a disentailment and a resettlement of the beneficial interests). Family interests under the trusts were revealed, and if these were by virtue of the Statute of Uses legal interests and had been assigned to third parties, might have to be carefully investigated. Both for the solicitor acting for the tenant for life, who was responsible for producing the abstract of title, and for the investigating solicitor, all this constituted an onerous task. Basically, then, the defect here was that the instruments creating and modifying the trusts formed the main documents in the first purchaser's title. These documents were not normally handed over to the purchaser on sale since they were likely to relate to other land in settlement, or to the creation of a subsisting trust or to the appointment or discharge of trustees of a subsisting trust (see Vendor and Purchaser Act 1874, s. 2, and now L.P.A. 1925, s. 45(9)). But the documents formed part of the title to the land for a number of years after the first sale and were liable to be produced by the person in whose possession they were, pursuant to an acknowledgment for production to that effect given to the first purchaser.

5. Overreaching effect of dealings

The draftsman's objective here was to give to the tenant for life (or other person equated by the Statute to his position) power to do something ostensibly quite beyond his powers. This was to convey the whole legal estate the subject of the settlement to the purchaser so that he obtained it free from the interests under the settlement. By the process known as *overreaching* these interests would then attach themselves to any capital money arising.

It is essential to appreciate that before 1926 in England, (and presently in Ireland) the life estate and fee tail were capable of subsisting as legal estates. The beneficial interests under the settlement would therefore subsist either at law or in equity, depending on the wording of the settlement. If the limitation was expressed in, say, 1882, as being "unto and to the use of X for life, remainder to the use of Y in tail, remainder to the use of Z in fee simple" X, Y and Z would obtain a legal life estate, fee tail and fee simple respectively. Had the limitation been rephrased as being "unto and to the use of T in fee simple in trust for A for life ..." etc. the beneficiaries would have obtained corresponding interests in equity. Whichever wording was chosen it will be noted that the tenant for life would either have an equitable interest or a *part* of the legal estate, never the whole legal estate.

By section 20 of the 1882 Act the purchaser's position is protected, in that a deed which affects to sell, exchange, partition, lease, mortgage or charge the land, to the extent which it can operate under the Act, "is effectual to pass the land conveyed ... discharged from all the limitations, powers, and provisions of the settlement." This effects the first half of the overreaching process, though the section goes on carefully to preserve estates prior to the settlement, and interests, charges, leases and other dispositions made by the tenant for life under his statutory powers.

The beneficiaries' position is equally protected by the second half of the overreaching process. By section 22(5), capital money arising or securities in which it is invested "shall, for all purposes of disposition, transmission and devolution, be considered as land, and the same shall be held for and go to the same persons successively, in the same manner ... as the land wherefrom the money arises would, if not disposed of, have been held and have gone under the settlement."

6. Flaws in the legislation

The 1882 Act was a neat conception. It was marred, however, by a number of minor flaws, many of which were remedied by the amending Acts. There were also three major flaws. One, the difficulty of making title, has already been discussed. The second was that it soon became apparent that there were several cases where though the land was indubitably settled, there was no one who was either a tenant for life or who could exercise the tenant for life's powers. A common case would be where the land was settled on discretionary trusts (see *e.g. Re Atkinson* (1886) 31 Ch.D. 577 and *Re Horne's Settled Estate* (1888) 39 Ch.D. 84). Since no beneficiary is *entitled* to any income, there was no one who came within section 58(*i*)(ix) of the 1882 Act, which is similar to section 20(i)(*viii*) of the 1925 Act. Other cases involved a direction to trustees to accumulate income until a beneficiary reached a specific age (see *Re Astor* [1922] 1 Ch. 364) or where there was a direction to pay a particular beneficiary a fixed annuity not equivalent to the whole income. In these cases, unless there was a trust for sale, the land could not be dealt with other than by joining all the beneficiaries in the conveyance *if* they were *sui juris*. This problem still exists where no remedial legislation has been passed, *e.g.* in Ireland (see Report of the Committee on the Registration of Title to Land in Northern Ireland (Cmgd. 512 (N.I.) (1967) para. 142(a) and *post*, Chapter 8). The third concerns trusts for sale.

7. The position of trusts for sale

By an addition added as an amendment to the original Bill a section was tacked on to the Act of 1882 (s. 63) deeming to be settled land any land "subject to a trust or direction for sale." This was no doubt intended to meet the not entirely groundless fear that "any conveyancer or lawyer would be able to defeat the best drawn scheme ... by vesting the real estate in trustees for sale" (Horace Davey, H.C. Deb. 1882, Vol. CCLXXII, Col. 360).

The effect of this was to give control of land settled by way of trust for sale not, as was normal, to the trustees responsible for executing the trust but to the tenant for life. The tenant for life was "the person for the time being beneficially entitled to the income of the land ... until sale" (s. 63). This legislative afterthought caused so much trouble and adverse comment (see 27 S.J. 113 and 28 S.J. 703) that the amending Act of 1884, introduced as its sponsor blandly explained to a not very sympathetic legislature "to remove a little friction which was found in the Act of last year," endeavoured to repair the position. A complete *volte face* was avoided and instead it was (a) made clear that in the ordinary way trustees for sale could execute the trusts without obtaining the tenant for life's consent (s. 6(1)) and (b) enacted by section 7 that the tenant for life could only exercise his powers over the land if he obtained leave of the court. Subsequent litigation suggested that such leave would be given if the tenant or tenants for life had a direct interest in the administration of the land and other parties would not be prejudiced (see *e.g. Re Harding's Estate* [1891] 1 Ch. 60).

The consequence was that it was vital for a purchaser to diagnose the nature of the settlement affecting the land he was buying. There were four possibilities. The settlement might be a formal strict settlement in which case the tenant for life would be responsible for making title. Secondly, the settlement might be a strict settlement except that the settlor had given the trustees a *power* of sale. The position here was that by a rather pusillanimous provision of the 1882 Act (s. 56(2)) the trustees could sell provided the tenant for life consented. (This provision was not repeated in the 1925 Act which makes any such attempt to confer on others the powers given by statute to the tenant for life nugatory by deeming them to be extra powers conferred on the tenant for life—see S.L.A. 1925, s. 108(2).) Thirdly the land could be settled by way of trust for sale in which case the trustees would sell *unless* the tenant for life had obtained an order in his favour which was duly registered as a *lis pendens* against the trustees. Fourthly, where there was a trust for sale but such an order was registered, the tenant for life would make title. Which of these categories a particular settlement fell into was not on occasion necessarily clear (and still sometimes is not clear after 1925). A trust for sale compulsorily postponed for a preliminary period was held not to be a trust for sale within section 63 (*Re Horne's Settled Estate* (1888) 39 Ch.D. 84), nor was a trust for sale revocable by or exercisable at the request of a beneficiary, (until that request was made) (*Re Goodall's Settlement* [1909] 1 Ch. 440). A trust "to retain or sell" might be construed either way (see *Re Johnson* [1915] 1 Ch. 435 and *Re White's Settlement* [1930] 1 Ch. 179). As has often been pointed out since, this position is most unsatisfactory since there is no doubt that either one or the other may sell. The only result is a wasteful litigation.

8. Powers of management under a trust for sale subject to the Settled Land Acts 1882-1890

It is important to appreciate that section 7 of the Act of 1884 removed powers from the tenant for life without conferring extra ones on the trustees. Trustees for sale found themselves without the necessary powers to manage (*i.e.* mortgage, lease, etc.) the land unless the trust instrument expressly conferred such process upon them. Thus in *Walker* v. *Southall* ((1887) 56 L.T. 882), North J. stated when considering the validity of mortgages effected by trustees for sale : "There is no case which goes further than to say that where there is a power (*sic*) of sale a mortgage may be justified by evidence of special circumstances which justified the raising of money in that way. Here there is the evidence of special circumstances" (at p. 883). Such exceptional circumstances might be found where *e.g.* a sheep farm is in danger of becoming a total loss because of being overrun with rabbits and general deterioration and is in need of substantial expenditure to make it saleable (see *Neill* v. *Neill* ([1904] 1 I.R. 513), an example of the court's salvage jurisdiction). Normally the general rule that a court will not rewrite a trust applies and either implied powers of management (see *Re Bellinger* ([1898] 2 Ch. 534), trustees for sale given power to make out of income or capital "any outlay which they might consider proper," held to include power to mortgage) or express powers. The only practicable way out of the problem was for the tenant for life to obtain an order under section 7 of the 1884 Act and then exercise the appropriate powers.

This most unsatisfactory position was remedied in England by section 28(1) of the Law of Property Act 1925 which conferred on trustees for sale all the powers of a tenant for life and the trustees of a settlement under the Settled Land Act 1925.

9. The Settled Land Act 1925

The Act of 1925, while by its Fifth Schedule repealing the Settled Land Act 1882-90, repeats the essence of the earlier legislation. Such alterations as were made are designed to improve the machinery of transactions with settled land rather than to make alterations of principle. It is perhaps a pity that a more draconian attempt at reform was not then made. For instance, a closer look might have been taken at a uniform method of settling land instead of preserving the two alternatives discussed above. An attempt might also have been made to "phase out" the entail. Both these ideas are discussed further later on in the book (see Chapter 8).

The long gestation which preceded the birth of the 1925 reforms is admirably summarised by Megarry and Wade (Chapter 19). Many of the ideas were originally those of Wolstenholme (see draft Conveyancing Bill of 1898) and the draftsman mainly concerned was Sir Benjamin Cherry, his pupil. Lord Haldane was responsible for Conveyancing Bills in 1913, 1914 and 1915 but reform was then postponed owing to the war. The legislation was first introduced as one huge Act, namely Sir Benjamin Cherry's Law of Property Act 1922, most of which was repealed and re-enacted in the Acts of 1925. The 1922 Act was preceded by the Fourth Report of the Acquisition and Valuation of Land Committee on the Transfer of Land in England and Wales (Cmd. 424 (1919)). This committee was chaired by Sir Leslie Scott and reported to the then Lord Chancellor, Lord Birkenhead. The Report explains that a pamphlet prepared by Arthur Underhill (senior conveyancing counsel of the court) was of great influence and offered "the best and simplest remedy to effect the required simplification with as little disturbance as possible." Benjamin Cherry was accordingly asked to prepare "a Bill on the lines indicated by Mr. Underhill" (para. 23).

Sir Arthur Underhill's pamphlet is entitled "The Line of

Least Resistance—An Easy but Effective Method of Simplifying the Law of Real Property," and is reproduced as Appendix I to the Fourth Report of the Scott Committee. It contains an excellent summary of the evolution of English land law framed in vigorous and clear terms. Its main proposal for reform is designed to remedy "the present chaotic state of the law" where there are "three systems of landholding: (1) the ancient patched up and incongruous freehold system, (2) the still more out of date copyhold system, and (3) the more modern leasehold system." The author's proposal was therefore, "to abolish all the complexities of the three systems above explained—*viz.* the freehold and copyhold tenures, and to ordain (in effect) that henceforth all land now held as freehold or copyhold shall have precisely the same legal incidents as if it were leasehold land holden for a term of, say, 100,000 years at a peppercorn rent." This, he explained, meant that every fee simple estate, whether freehold or copyhold, and whether in possession, reversion or remainder should for all purposes "have all the incidents of a chattel real estate, save only that they shall continue in perpetuity and not merely for a term of years certain and that may be called freehold estates in fee simple to distinguish them from estates for years certain." The attraction of this idea as regards successive interests was that leaseholds were not affected by the Statute of Uses or the statutes *De Donis Conditionalibus* or *Quia Emptores*. They could not therefore be entailed and could only be settled by way of a trust, just as for stocks and shares. Furthermore leaseholds devolved as personalty prior to 1926 and were not affected by the law of primogeniture.

To the charge that this suggestion was unscientific, Underhill replied:

"Some of my friends have objected that this scheme is unscientific and the intervention of a rank opportunist. But our law is not scientific; and a people that can persuade itself with ease that it is noontide on a summer's day when the sun still bears 15 degrees East of South is not likely to object to the enactment that freehold land shall have all the incidents of a long leasehold on the ground that it is unscientific. Moreover, would it be any more unscientific than abolishing our complicated system of weights and measures and substituting the metric system?"

Unscientific or not, Underhill's concept, though formulated in the 1925 legislation in a rather different way to the one he suggested, forms the key to the understanding of the reforms.

On the mechanism of the simplification of title to settled land, Underhill's detailed suggestions are well worth reproducing, for they remain enshrined in the Settled Land Act 1925:

"It is conceded that the proposed conversion of freeholds and copyholds into perpetual leaseholds, while rationalising and simplifying the law, would not by itself simplify (and as a corollary cheapen) the practice of conveyancing so far as settled property is concerned, because it would still be necessary to investigate all the trusts of settlements so as to judge whether the person who is purporting to deal with the property is empowered to do so, either under the provisions of the settlement, or as a person having the statutory powers of a tenant for life under the Settled Land Acts. I have been seriously told that the British Bolshevist is so concerned at the cost of investigating titles that there is danger of a revolution, or at least of a "general strike" in consequence. It has always appeared to me, however, that he was exclusively interested in obtaining land without any payment or compensation, and that the costs of employing a solicitor to investigate the victim's title neither has entered nor could enter into his calculations. No doubt that would be so, unless some alterations in the law were made, because, as matters stand, whenever a purchaser has notice of a trust he is bound to see that the transaction with him is authorised by that trust.

Now there are two ways of dealing with this question. The first and simplest would be to follow the practice with regard to settled stocks and shares, *viz.* vest the legal ownership in trustees, and keep all notice of trusts off the ownership title. In the case of stocks the ownership is proved by an entry in the Company's register, and no notification of trusts is allowed. No inconvenience is caused in such cases, because the ownership of stocks confers no such desirable social rights as does the ownership of land. But if settled land were to be placed on the same basis, and if purchasers and lessees were (as would be the essence of such a scheme) to be restricted to dealing with the trustees, two difficulties would have to be faced, *viz.*; (1) The trustees, and not the beneficial life tenant would have to be the legal landlords; all leases would have to be made in their names. All rent would have to be paid to them, and all breaches of covenant by the tenants would have to be sued for in their names. Actions for trespasses and other injuries to the land would have to be taken in their names. The beneficial tenant for life would, in fact, be reduced to the position of an annuitant. (2) Such a system would be altogether contrary to the policy of the Settled Land Acts, which (as stated above) was to place beneficial tenants for life and other persons in analogous situations in the position of trustees for their successors, and to confer upon them large statutory powers of selling, leasing, and, in proper cases, mortgaging the settled land while safeguarding the material interests of their successors by causing all capital money arising from sale or mortgage to be paid either to the trustees or into Court.

This policy was intended not merely for the benefit of the persons interested under the settlement, but also of the tenants of the land, so as to give the beneficial owner for the time being a free hand in its development and management, and it is, therefore, hopeless to dream of reversing it by vesting all rights in trustees, with whom alone third parties should henceforth deal.

That being so, how is the difficulty to be met?

My suggestion as to this is a simplification of an ingenious scheme elaborated in Lord Haldane's Conveyancing Bill of

1913. Substantially this scheme provides that the entire fee simple or terms of years which is the subject of the settlement is to be conveyed from time to time to each successive tenant for life or in tail as and when he becomes entitled to possession. He would thus become the ostensible absolute legal owner, although in reality only a trustee for himself and his successors. In order to prevent a tenant for life from dealing with the estate and pocketing the proceeds so as to injure his successors, the scheme would provide that the instrument conveying the property to him should contain an appointment of trustees for the purposes of the Settled Land Acts, and (if the settlement so allows) it must also contain provisions extending the powers of the Settled Land Acts. The appointment of Settled Land Act trustees would act as a danger signal, intimating to purchasers, mortgagees and others that the ostensible legal owner is really a trustee whose powers are limited to those conferred by the Settled Land Acts as extended (if at all) by the conveyance in question. The settlement itself is to be kept off the title, and is in no way to affect or concern a purchaser, mortgagee, or lessee. The document in fact vesting the estate in a tenant for life in possession creates in favour of a purchaser, mortgagee, or lessee what may be called a certified tenant for life capable of exercising the powers of the Settled Land Acts, and such extension (if any) of those powers as the instrument may contain, and also creating certified trustees of the settlement for the purposes of the Settled Land Acts, to whom all capital money arising from such sales and mortgages would have to be paid.

All that a purchaser, mortgagee, or lessee would be bound to do would be to satisfy himself that the proposed transaction with him fell within; (1) the statutory powers of a tenant for life as (2) extended (if at all) by the conveyance to the certified life tenant. By this means the title to real and leasehold estates would be greatly simplified and shortened, consisting wholly of simple conveyances and mortgages; for on the death of each successive life tenant or tenant in tail his executors or administrators would simply convey the estate to the next person beneficially entitled to the possession (if a person falling within the Settled Land Acts), or, if not, then to the trustees of the settlement or the person absolutely entitled. . . .

If the criticism be made that this scheme is highly artificial, inasmuch as it enables a person to pose as owner for purposes of sale, leasing, etc., who is not the real owner, the answer is that Parliament has already accepted the idea in relation to registration of title, as the Registrar invariably registers a tenant for life as the statutory proprietor.

Moreover, all that it comes to is this, that in settlements of land you must have two sets of trustees; one, the trustee of the land itself, who must always be the person or persons to whom the Settled Land Acts give powers of sale and leasing, and the other the trustees of capital moneys arising from sales, etc."

CHAPTER 4

THE STRUCTURE OF THE SETTLED LAND ACT 1925

THE following represents a summary of the main structural points of the 1925 Act, particular emphasis being placed on provisions changing or extending the policy of the 1882 Act.

1. The position of the tenant for life

Before 1926 the overreaching effect of dealings by the tenant for life was secured by a provision in the 1882 Act stating that the tenant for life's conveyance was effective to pass the whole estate in the land free from all the limitations under the settlement (see *ante*, p. 37).

Apparently more logical is the scheme of the 1925 Act which secures the vesting in the limited owner the fee simple absolute in possession (or the entire term of years if the land settled is leasehold) (s. 4(2)). Where there are two or more persons of full age entitled for life as joint tenants they together constitute the tenant for life (s. 19(2)). It was held in *Re 90 Thornhill Road, Tolworth, Surrey*; *Barker* v. *Addiscott* ([1969] 3 W.L.R. 570) that one joint tenant could not obtain an order that the other should join in to exercise the power of sale. Where there were powers, joint or otherwise, the court would not interfere and direct them to be exercised in the absense of mala fides. As before, the primary protection given to the beneficiaries is that the tenant for life is a trustee of his powers (s. 107(1)) and in addition he holds the settled land itself upon trust to give effect to the equitable interests and powers affecting the land (s. 16(1)).

Rather less logical is, having vested in him the entire legal estate, to confer express powers upon him as if he were not so entitled. Furthermore these powers are significantly less than those of an unlimited owner (see *post*, p. 62).

2. Where tenant for life is an infant

Before 1926 in England (and at present in Ireland) an infant could hold a legal estate in land, but because no purchaser would deal with an infant who was by law inalienably entitled to revoke the transaction on attaining his majority or within a reasonable time thereafter (see *ante*, p. 33) the land was deemed to be settled land. The infant was deemed to be tenant for life but his powers were exercisable on his behalf by the trustees of the settlement (S.L.A. 1882, ss. 59, 60).

The 1925 Act changed the position only as far as was necessary to maintain consistency with the principle that an infant cannot after 1925 hold a legal estate in land (L.P.A. 1925, s. 1(6)). The legal estate as well as the statutory powers are, therefore, normally vested in the trustees of the settlement (S.L.A. 1925, s. 26(1)). Section 27 states that the effect of a conveyance of a legal estate in land to an infant operates as an agreement for valuable consideration to execute a settlement in favour of the infant.

3. Other limited owners

The 1925 Act follows the scheme laid down in 1882 of equating other limited owners to the tenant for life. Thus, for example, tenants in tail, tenants in fee simple subject to gifts over and tenants for years terminable on life have the powers of a tenant for life (s. 20). Since the definition of those with the powers of a tenant for life must be complementary to the definition of settled land it was necessary to make one innovation to cater for the position where land was deemed to be settled land for the first time. As will be seen, the case in question was where land was charged with the payment of certain charges of a family nature. There is consequently included within the list in section 20 "a person beneficially entitled to land for an estate in fee simple or for a term of years absolute subject to any estates, interests, charges, or powers of charging, subsisting or capable of being exercised under a settlement" (s. 20(1)(ix)).

4. Where there is no tenant for life

Here the 1925 Act, by a simple provision, greatly improved upon the pre-1926 position where there was no one qualified to exercise the powers of a tenant for life (discussed *ante*, p. 38). Now, where there is no tenant for life because *e.g.* the trust is a discretionary one where no one is *entitled* to the income or where the trust involves a preliminary period during which the income is accumulated, the legal estate in the land and the statutory powers are vested in the "statutory owner." The statutory owner is constituted by the trustees of the settlement unless the settlement expressly confers the powers upon someone of full age (ss. 23, 117(1)(xxvi)).

5. The trustees

(a) Identity

The 1925 Act reproduced the list of those persons competent to act as trustees in the same priority as that in the Settled Land Acts 1882-90, but added one useful extra category. The procedure involves going down the list in the set order until persons in the appropriate category are found. The list runs (s. 30), in summarised form:

(i) The persons *with power of sale* of settled land,

(ii) The persons *declared by the settlement* to be trustees thereof for the purpose of the Settled Land Act 1925 (or its predecessors),

(iii) The persons under the settlement *with power of* or *upon trust for sale of other land* subject to the same limitations (or power of consent to or approval of such power),

(iv) The persons with a *future power of sale or who are future trustees for sale* (or with power or consent to or approval of such future power),

(v) The persons appointed by those *beneficiaries* who to-gether would be able to dispose of the settled land in equity for the whole estate the subject of the settlement.

The new residual provision caters for the position where the settlement is created by will (or arises by reason of an intestacy). If there are no trustees appointed then the personal representatives of the deceased are the trustees of the settle-ment, and if there is only one personal representative he is obliged to appoint another person to act as trustee with him (s. 30(3)).

A word should be said about two traps implicit in the above. The first is that it will be seen that heading the list are persons with power of sale of the settled land. After 1925 such power is, of course, unconditionally vested in the tenant for life, but the purported conferring of such a power (if a general power) on persons other than the tenant for life suffices to make them trustees. This is completely illogical in present day conditions, and is a direct result of the pre-1883 practice of empowering the trustees to sell or consent to a sale. The Settled Land Act 1882 had, of course, to deal with existing settlements and it was then logical to give priority to such persons. The other trap lies in the second provision conferring the position of trustee upon the persons "who are by the settlement declared to be trustees thereby for the purposes of the Settled Land Acts." In *Re Bentley* ((1885) 54 L.J. Ch. 782) an appointment of two persons merely as "trustees" was held insufficient to make them trustees of the settled land.

(b) Referential and compound settlements

By a new provision, trustees of referential settlements (a settlement of one property by reference to the trusts of an existing settlement of another property) are, in the absence of a fresh appointment in the later settlement, the trustees of the settlement to which reference is made (s. 32).

In the case of compound settlements, particular difficulty

was apt to be encountered before 1926 with regard to over-reaching. If a tenant for life was tenant for life under both the original settlement and a resettlement, the only way that the interests under both settlements could be overreached and any larger powers conferred by the resettlement exercised was by selling as tenant for life under the compound settlement (the compound settlement being a separate entity from the settlement and resettlement). Selling as tenant for life under the original settlement would overreach the interests under both settlements, but no larger powers conferred by the resettlement could be exercised. Selling as tenant for life of the resettlement did not overreach the interests, such as portions, which might still exist under the original settlement (and this was so even if the new life interest was expressed to be in restoration and by way of confirmation of the old) until in December 1925 the decision in *Parr* v. *Att.-Gen.* ([1926] A.C. 239) reversed the law as previously understood (see now s. 22(2) retrospectively confirming this decision). Sales by tenants for life under compound settlements were rare since they depended upon the existence of compound trustees. Compound trustees could probably not be validly appointed either by the original settlement or by the resettlement, and could consequently only be brought into existence by consent of all the beneficiaries (assuming they were *sui juris*) or by a court appointment. Section 31 now solves this rather artificial difficulty by providing, in effect, that the trustees of the original settlement, or if there are none, of the resettlement, are trustees of the compound settlement.

6. Definition of settled land

The simple definition contained in section 2(5) of the 1882 Act (*ante*, p. 33) was considerably enlarged in the parallel provision in the 1925 Act. As has already been pointed out, it was necessary to make the definition of settled land dovetail with the definition of the tenant for life or other limited owner having his powers.

By section 2, land which is or is deemed to be the subject

of a settlement is for the purposes of the Act settled land. Section 1 defined what constitutes a settlement, and states:

"1.—(1) Any deed, will, agreement for a settlement or other agreement, Act of Parliament, or other instrument, or any number of instruments, whether made or passed before or after, or partly before and partly after, the commencement of this Act, under or by virtue of which instrument or instruments any land, after the commencement of this Act, stands for the time being—

 (i) limited in trust for any persons by way of succession; or
 (ii) limited in trust for any person in possession—

  (*a*) for an entailed interest whether or not capable of being barred or defeated;
  (*b*) for an estate in fee simple or for a term of years absolute subject to an executory limitation, gift, or disposition over on failure of his issue or in any other event;
  (*c*) for a base or determinable fee or any corresponding interest in leasehold land;
  (*d*) being an infant, for an estate in fee simple or for a term of years absolute; or

 (iii) limited in trust for any person for an estate in fee simple or for a term of years absolute contingently on the happening of any event; or
 (iv) [Repealed by the Married Women (Restraint upon Anticipation) Act 1949].
 (v) charged, whether voluntarily or in consideration of marriage or by way of family arrangement, and whether immediately or after an interval, with the payment of any rentcharge for the life of any person, or any less period, or of any capital, annual, or periodical sums for the portions, advancement, maintenance, or otherwise for the benefit of any persons, with or without any term of years for securing or raising the same;

creates or is for the purposes of this Act a settlement and is in this Act referred to as a settlement, or as the settlement, as the case requires."

The following points are worth noting concerning the drafting and implications of this section:

(a) By section 1(1) of the Law of Property Act 1925 the only estates in land which are capable of existing as legal estates are an estate in fee simple absolute in possession and a term of years absolute. It therefore follows that where *e.g.* a fee simple is less than absolute or not in possession (because there is a succession of interests) the less than absolute or future interest must subsist behind a trust. Similarly an infant cannot hold a legal estate after 1925. The word "limited," however, implies an active limitation by the settlor and seems inappropriate to describe, for instance, a devise to "X in tail," a limitation simply "to X for life" with a resulting trust to the donor or, indeed, a straightforward purported conveyance to an infant (as to which, see s. 27). The same point was recently taken by Lord Denning in *Binions* v. *Evans* ([1972] 2 All E.R. 70) when, referring to a document purporting to create a tenancy at will, he dismissed the suggestion that the document in question created a settlement. He stated that "this land may be held on trust ... but it is not 'limited' in trust (which I take to be expressly limited)" (at p. 74). Accordingly the Northern Ireland redraft of the 1925 legislation (referred to in more detail *post*, p. 138) omits the word "limited" and refers instead to cases where the land is "held on trust for any persons by way of succession" (Draft Property Bill, cl. 22). The statutory phrase, incidentally, is general enough to catch, without the need for specific mention, interests set out in section 1(1)(ii)(*a*) to (*c*) of the 1925 Act, the element of succession in, for instance, an entail being the reversion or remainder taking effect after the entail.

(b) Land "limited in trust for any person for an estate in fee simple or for a term of years absolutely contingently on the happening of any event" will be held for a "springing interest." Usually this will involve a succession of interests but this will not necessarily be so (*e.g.* devise to the testator's first son to marry, the intermediate income to be accumulated and appropriated to capital). Shifting interests (*e.g.* a devise to A in fee simple provided that if he fails to provide a home for his mother there then the house is to go to B in fee simple) are covered by section 1(1)(ii)(*b*).

(c) For the first time land subject to "family charges" which would normally consist of jointures for widows or portions for children (but including all annual or other charges of a "family" rather than "commercial" character) was made settled land by section 1(1)(v). Formerly only if the family charges were to arise in the future was the land settled under the Act of 1882 (see *Re Lord Wimborne & Browne* [1904] 1 Ch. 537, 541). Otherwise if there was no element of succession the land was not settled (see *Re Carnarvon's (Earl) Settled Estates* [1927] 1 Ch. 138, 155). The common practice was, therefore, to sell the land in such a way that either the owners of the charges joined in the conveyance to release them in return for a proportion of the proceeds of sale or the land was conveyed to the purchaser subject to the charges but with the vendor's indemnity against them. The change of policy whereby such land was suddenly declared settled by section 1(1)(v) caused many difficulties. The original settlement creating the charges would in some circumstances obtain a new lease of life and the trustees thereunder would be revived at the same time, although the land might have ceased to be settled for some time. A purchaser who had bought subject to the charges but otherwise would assume that he was the unfettered owner would find that a vesting deed must be executed in his favour and his powers over the land were as laid down by the Act. To mitigate these difficulties the Law of Property (Amendment) Act 1926 (s. 1(1)) gave owners of land subject to family charges the option of putting the clock back to before 1926 and selling the land as if it were unsettled, with an indemnity as before but without a vesting deed. Although this is

theoretically attractive, it must be pointed out that in practice
the purchase of land subject to charges of this sort and with
the protection merely of a personal indemnity by the vendor
is not an attractive proposition. Normally the purchaser would
insist on the charges being overreached by the Settled Land
Act procedure being followed (or perhaps by a conveyance
first to trustees for sale appointed for the purpose of overreaching, on a sale by them, equities existing prior to the
creation of the trust under the rarely used section 2(2) of the
Law of Property Act 1925). Alternatively it is often simpler
for the vendor to get the charges discharged and bring the
settlement to an end prior to sale.

(d) Restraints on anticipation were abolished in 1949 but
were important in former years. An effective restraint prevented a *married* woman from disposing of or charging the
capital or future income of property vested in her for her
separate use. As this would produce a case of "land in fetters,"
such land was deemed to be settled under the former section
1(1)(iv).

(e) Dower assigned by metes and bounds (a widow's one-
third part of a specific piece of land enjoyed for life, which
can only arise in rare cases since it was abolished in the case
of a person dying after 1926 by the Administration of
Estates Act 1925) produces a notional settlement. The document creating the settlement is the letters of administration
or probate to the deceased husband's estate (s. 1(3)).

(f) By a very important afterthought, land held upon trust
for sale is declared not to be settled land (s. 1(7), added by
the Law of Property (Amendment) Act 1926).

7. Conveyancing procedure

As has been demonstrated (*ante*, p. 46) Underhill's idea was
to create a "certified tenant for life" and a set of "certified
trustees" so that "the title to real and leasehold estates would
be greatly simplified and shortened, consisting wholly of
simple conveyances and mortgages." This policy is imple-
mented in the following way:

(a) Two documents

After 1925 all settlements (other than those upon an immediate binding trust for sale) must be made by two documents. Basically, one document declares the trusts on which the land is to be held and appoints the trustees, whereas the other operates as a conveyance to the tenant for life (or declaration that the legal estate is vested in him on trust if he was the settlor).

Section 4(3) states that the trust instrument shall:

    (a) declare the trusts;
    (b) appoint the trustees of the settlement;
    (c) contain the power, if any, to appoint new trustees;
    (d) set out any powers in extension of those conferred by the Act;
    (e) bear any stamp duty.

Section 5(1) states that the vesting deed shall contain:

    (a) a description of the settled land;
    (b) a statement that the settled land is vested in the person to be whom it is conveyed or in whom it is declared to be vested upon the trusts affecting the settled land;
    (c) the names of the trustees of the settlement;
    (d) any additional or larger powers conferred by the trust instrument;
    (e) the name of any person entitled to appoint new trustees.

Section 6 states that where the land is settled by will, the will is for the purposes of the Act the trust instrument. The personal representatives hold the land on trust to execute a vesting instrument in favour of the tenant for life or statutory owner and this instrument will normally be a vesting *assent*, a document similar to the vesting deed but not under seal. (For an example of the working of the scheme where an entail is created by will, see *ante*, 14 *et seq*. and in a more straightforward case, *post*, p. 67.)

The "certified tenant for life" scheme works in this way
once the settlement is correctly established. Suppose that
under an existing settlement the land stands limited to A for
life, remainder to B for life, remainder to C in fee simple.
When A dies the land devolves upon the *special personal
representatives* of A. These will be the trustees of the land
unless the testator appoints them expressly (Administration
of Estates Act 1925, s. 22(1)). These special representatives
will take out a grant of probate limited to the settled land,
the rest of the testator's "free" (*i.e.* unsettled) estate devolving
in the normal way upon his general personal representatives.
Having obtained probate, the special representatives will
execute a vesting assent as described above in favour of B
(Settled Land Act 1925, s. 7, which deals generally with
change of ownership). When B dies the settlement comes to
an end and C becomes absolutely entitled to the land. The
legal estate is then conveyed to C by B's *general* personal
representatives (*Re Bridgett and Hayes' Contract* [1928] Ch.
163). To summarise, the general scheme of section 7 is to
oblige the person or persons in whom the legal estate is
vested, whether trustees, personal representatives or a previous
tenant for life whose interest has ceased under the terms of
the settlement, to convey the legal estate to the newly qualified
tenant for life.

(b) *Evasion of the Act*

Section 13, (as amended by Law of Property (Am.) Act 1926)
the "paralysing section," provides for the case where no vesting deed is executed. Where a tenant for life is entitled to have
a vesting deed or assent executed in his favour then until
this is done no disposition of the land can take effect (except
by a personal representative or in favour of a purchaser
without notice of the tenant for life having become so entitled).
A purported disposition operates only as a contract for
valuable consideration to carry out the transaction after the
requisite vesting instrument has been executed, and this must
be registered as a land charge.

(c) *Investigation of title and conveyance*

Normally a purchaser from the tenant for life will merely be concerned with tracing the devolution of the legal estate to the vendor-tenant for life. Title might have to be traced back to and beyond the settlor where the settlement is recent but the settlor's trust instrument will be ignored. Title may even consist of a series of vesting deeds or assents which are regarded as good roots of title. The fact that the scheme envisages that the vesting instrument must be a "certificate" to the purchaser involves obliging him to assume that the statements relating to the identity of the tenant for life, the trustees and relating to the other statutory matters are true (s. 110(2)). All the purchaser must do is to pay the purchase money to the certified trustees and the legal estate can then be validly conveyed to him by the tenant for life. The *equitable* interests arising under the settlement, of which he should have no direct knowledge, are overreached, but *prior* legal estates, and mortgages and leases created by the tenant for life, are *not* overreached (s. 72). Conversely, certain non-commercial interests created prior to the settlement, *viz.* annuities, limited owner's charges and general equitable charges are overreached even if protected by registration (s. 72(3)). This facilitates "clean titles" and does not unduly prejudice the owners of these family charges, who would after the sale own parallel interests in money. In the case of a sale under a specially created *"ad hoc"* settlement certain other increasingly obsolete equitable interests are overreached— *e.g.* a widow's right of dower not assigned by metes and bounds (s. 21).

Exceptionally the purchaser must also investigate the trust instrument. Section 110(2) provides a few such cases, the more usual of which being where the settlement existed before 1926 or where the proper formalities have not been used to effect a settlement. Here the purchaser must check that (a) the land to be conveyed is subject to the settlement, (b) that the tenant for life is the true tenant for life and (c) that the trustees are properly constituted.

(d) *The end of the settlement*

In the simple case of where a life interest is given to A for
life with remainder to B in fee simple the settlement comes
to an end as described above (see p. 58) *i.e.* on A's death
his general personal representatives will vest the legal estate
in B by an ordinary assent, and B can require them to do so
(s. 7(5)). But how does a purchaser from B know that the
settlement came to an end on A's death? The answer is that
a purchaser is bound to assume that the settlement has come
to an end and that the vendor is "absolutely and beneficially"
entitled provided the assent in favour of B "does not state
who are the trustees of the settlement for the purposes of
this Act" (s. 110(5)). Unfortunately section 18 complicates
the issue by stating that if the land has been subject to a
vesting instrument an unauthorised disposition will be void
as regards the legal estate. Thus if the land in fact remains
settled on A's death, because *e.g.* there are outstanding family
charges in favour of C, the conveyance to B's purchaser
would be void. In practice, though, if the land has been vested
in B by a clean assent by general personal representatives,
this is accepted and section 110(5) relied upon. (See also
Wolstenholme and Cherry's *Conveyancing Statutes,* pp. 67,
229.)

In certain other cases a deed of discharge is needed to
evidence the end of the settlement. This is a deed declaring
that the trustees are discharged from their duties, and is
evidence to a purchaser from a person absolutely entitled to
land formerly settled that the land is not settled. An example
of its use was mentioned in Chapter 2 (*ante*, p. 16) where the
tenant in tail disentailed and the trustees evidenced the consequential termination of the settlement by a deed of discharge
under section 17. A deed of discharge must therefore be used
in all cases where (a) there has been a vesting deed and (b)
there is no subsequent conveyance or assent which does not
contain a statement of the names of the Settled Land Act
trustees (*e.g.* usually, where the settlement has ended
otherwise than on death). The theory is that the pur-

chaser, having had notice of the existence of trusts in the vesting deed must now have a statutory guarantee that those trusts no longer exist. It was held in *Re Alefounder's Will Trusts* ([1927] 1 Ch. 360) that where a tenant in tail disentailed before a vesting deed was executed, he could sell the land without first obtaining a vesting deed. It follows, therefore, that no deed of discharge would be needed either. Other cases sometimes met where a deed of discharge is necessary are (a) where land ceases to be settled on an infant attaining majority (though in practice the land is often, if appropriate, allowed to remain vested in personal representatives until this event and then is conveyed by them by simple assent to the former infant), (b) where the tenant for life who has obtained a vesting deed purchases the remainder, and (c) where a tenant for life holds land subject to family charges which now cease to burden the land.

(e) Registered land

Finally, in view of the ever-increasing pace of registration of title, how the title to settled land is dealt with on the register must be mentioned. The Settled Land Act 1925 applies to land the title to which is registered, but by section 119(3) the Act takes effect subject to the provisions of the Land Registration Act 1925 (and the Rules made thereunder). Just as the trust instrument is "off the title" it is also "off the Register." When a settlement is made, the legal estate is vested in the tenant for life by (a) the execution of a vesting transfer in the style of Form 21 in the Schedule to the Land Registration Rules and (b) the name of the tenant for life being registered in the proprietorship register (Land Registration Act 1925, s. 86(1)). Overreachable interests of beneficiaries under the settlement take effect as minor interests and are protected by restrictions entered on the register (s. 86(2)(3) *ibid*). Thus, where the tenant for life is registered as proprietor, the following restriction will appear under his registration:

"No disposition under which capital money arises is to be
registered unless the money is paid to AB of etc. and CD
of etc. (the trustees of the settlement) or into Court.
Except under an order of the Registrar, no disposition is
to be registered unless authorised by the Settled Land Act
1925."

The pattern of the Settled Land Act 1925 is faithfully
adapted to the title registration system so that the tenant for
life or statutory owner always appears as proprietor, the
entries on the register (including the appropriate restrictions)
serving the same function as the vesting deed. The settlement
itself may be filed in the registry (without prejudice to its still
being officially "off the Register") and the registrar has a
useful power to certify that an intended disposition is
authorised by the settlement and will be registered (Land
Registration Act 1925, ss. 88, 89).

8. Powers of tenant for life

Central to the policy of the Settled Land Acts 1882-90 and
the Settled Land Act 1925 were two principles. The first was
that it should be the tenant for life or the limited owner in
possession who should normally exercise the powers given
or authorised by statute. The second principle, established to
stop the problems caused by the compromises made by the
Settled Estates Act 1856, was that these powers could not
be taken away, curtailed or their exercise inhibited by
provisions in the settlement, any such provision being void
(see S.L.A. 1882, ss. 50-52; S.L.A. 1925, s. 106). The problems
to which these provisions have occasionally given rise are
discussed in Chapter 6. It remains now to state what the
powers are and to show how the 1925 Act extended them.
The following chart summarises the position.

Main Powers Normally Exercisable by Limited Owner Affecting Legal Estate	Settled Land Acts 1882-90	Settled Land Act 1925
(1) *Sale* of settled land or any right over it, or *exchange* of the settled land.	Yes, by auction or private contract provided sold at best price that can reasonably be obtained (ss. 3, 4).	Yes, subject to conditions similar to those imposed in 1882; a rent may in addition be reserved on the sale (ss. 38-40).
(2) *Dealings with principal mansion house* and land enjoyed therewith.	No, unless consent of trustees or court order is obtained. Farmhouses or houses on sites not exceeding 25 acres not deemed "principal mansion houses" (S.L.A. 1890, s. 10).	Yes, provided either the settlement was made before 1926 and does not provide to the contrary, or, if the settlement is post-1925 it does not expressly require trustees' consent or a court order (s. 65(1)). (Similar definition of "principal mansion house" to that in S.L.A. 1882-90).
(3) *Leasing* settled land.	Yes, the length of the term being limited by the purpose: Building Leases — 99 years Mining Leases — 60 years Other Leases — 21 years Leases to be granted subject to various conditions, including that they be made by deed and reserve best rent reasonably obtainable. Power for court to extend terms authorised (S.L.A. 1882, ss. 6-11, 65(10)).	Yes, the length of the lease being limited by the purpose: Building or Forestry Leases—999 years Mining Leases —100 years Other Leases —50 years These lengths apply after 1925 whenever the settlement was made, but the leases must be made subject to similar conditions as imposed by S.L.A. 1882-90 (ss. 41-48).

Main Powers Normally Exercisable by Limited Owner Affecting Legal Estate	Settled Land Acts 1882-90	Settled Land Act 1925
(4) Grant of *options* to sell or lease the settled land.	No, except if contained in a building lease, or agreement to grant one, and the price or rent being the best reasonably obtainable and the option being exercisable within ten years (S.L.A. 1889, ss. 2, 3).	Yes, if in writing, the grant of the option being subject to similar conditions to those laid down by the Act of 1889 (s. 51).
(5) To *mortgage*.	No, except for limited purposes, *i.e.* equality of exchange or partition, or for discharging incumbrances (S.L.A. 1882, s. 18; S.L.A. 1890, s. 11).	No, except for limited purposes (rather wider than under the Acts of 1882-90). These include for raising money to give effect to the terms of the settlement and purposes beneficial to the settled land such as discharging incumbrances or paying for improvements (ss. 16, 71).
(6) To *improve*.	No, unless a scheme is first approved by trustees or court proposing improvements within statutory list (*e.g.* for drainage, irrigation, road-making, sewerage). Improvements may then be paid for out of capital money in hand (S.L.A. 1882, ss. 25-29; S.L.A. 1890, ss. 13-15).	Yes, improvements are within wider statutory list and improvements are certified as having been properly done (but no need for a prior scheme). Less permanent improvements may be paid for out of capital but the tenant for life must repay by instalments (ss. 84-89).

Other subsidiary powers include power to cut and sell timber. If the tenant for life is impeachable of waste he must obtain the consent of the trustees or a court order and three-quarters of the sale proceeds must be appropriated to capital. If unimpeachable, no consent is needed and the proceeds belong to him (S.L.A. 1925, s. 66). He also has power to compromise claims with the trustees' written consent (s. 58(1)) and to sell settled chattels if he obtains a court order (s. 67), the proceeds being capital money. An important power, sometimes overlooked, is the power to select investments for capital money within any of the wide range stipulated by section 73 of the 1925 Act as extended, if appropriate by the settlement (s. 75, and compare Act of 1882, ss. 21 and 22(2) to similar effect). Finally, a useful power is given for the tenant for life himself to acquire the settled land, though in this case the trustees must act in his name on his behalf (s. 68).

The formalities regarding the exercise of his powers are these. Where the tenant for life wishes to lease the settled land and it is at the best rent reasonably obtainable, no notice to the trustees need be given if the term is for not more than twenty-one years. In most cases, including sales and longer leases, the tenant for life must give written notice by registered post, at least one month before the transaction becomes binding, to the trustees, and their solicitor if known (s. 101). However, a person dealing in good faith with the tenant for life is not concerned to enquire as to whether such notice has been given (s. 101(5)) and section 97 gives to the trustees a wide indemnity in respect of inaction, or indeed for giving consents or adopting contracts. Furthermore, except where the tenant for life intends to mortgage or charge the land, the notice can be a general one stating that he intends to exercise his Settled Land Act powers, though he must furnish further particulars if so required by the trustees (s. 101(2) and (3)). In a few cases the trustees' consent is required (e.g. sale of principal mansion house) and these cases have been mentioned above.

For the protection of purchasers from the tenant for life, if they deal in good faith with him they are conclusively

taken to have given the best price, consideration or rent and
to have complied with the requirements of the Act (section
110(1), a protection generously interpreted in *Re Morgan's
Lease* [1972] Ch. 1, see *post*, p. 94).

Although these formalities in most cases afford a rather
nominal protection to the settlement beneficiaries, serious
misfeasance by the tenant for life is made very difficult by the
provision that all capital money arising on any transaction
(*e.g.* sale proceeds, proceeds of mortgage, premium on a lease)
must be paid to between two and four trustees (or one if a
trust corporation (s. 94(1)). If this is not done, the beneficial
interests under the settlement will not be overreached and the
purchaser's title will be severely defective. Alternatively, the
capital money may be paid into court (s. 18(1)(*b*)).

In addition to these specific powers, the court has a general
jurisdiction under section 64 to authorise any transaction by
the tenant for life which would be for the benefit of the settled
land, if it is one which an absolute owner could have effected.
The word "transaction" has been liberally construed. A scheme
to raise money to pay the debts of the tenant for life incurred
in the upkeep of the estate, repayment to be made on the life
tenant's death was approved in *Re White-Popham Estates*
([1936] Ch. 725) despite the benefit being to the persons
interested under the settlement rather than to the settled land
(and see also *Re Scarisbrick Re-Settlement Estates* [1944]
Ch. 229). The re-arrangement of beneficial interests to
minimise taxation has also been held to be a "transaction"
within the section (*Re Downshire Settled Estates* [1953] Ch.
218) and the section thus forms a valuable supplement to the
"trust-busting" jurisdiction of the court under the Variation
of Trusts Act 1958. In *Re Simmons* ([1956] Ch. 125) it was
held that if the settlement was by way of trust for sale, a
similar jurisdiction to that conferred on the court by section
64 existed.

Finally, the Act deals with the situation where the tenant
for life has ceased to have a substantial interest in the settled
land and unreasonably refuses to exercise his powers. In this

case any person interested may apply to the court for an order authorising the trustees to exercise the powers on the behalf of and in the name of the tenant for life (s. 24; see *Re Thornhill's Settlement* ([1941] Ch. 24-tenant for life bankrupt and unreasonably refused to sell requisitioned land to War Office. Order made to enable trustees to do this). The position under section 24 should not be confused with the position where the tenant for life has assured his interest with intent to extinguish it to the person next entitled under the settlement. Here under section 105, the statutory powers become exercisable as if the tenant for life whose interest is extinguished were dead.

9. Land vested in charities

By section 29, all land vested in trustees on or for charitable, ecclesiastical, or public trusts or purposes is deemed to be settled land and the trustees have all the powers conferred by the Act on the tenant for life and trustees of a settlement. The section makes it clear that a separate instrument is not necessary in this case to give effect to the settlement except where the settlement is created by a post-1925 will. It was, also, held in *In Re Booth* ([1927] 1 Ch. 579) that this section makes charity land settled land only so as to confer on the trustees the Settled Land Act powers, and not further or otherwise.

10. Practical illustration of the working of the Act

Suppose that John Brown makes the following will, dated December 6, 1971:

THIS IS THE LAST WILL AND TESTAMENT of me JOHN BROWN of Sootyacre, Blacktown, Staffordshire.

1. I appoint my brother Charles Brown and my solicitor Josiah Snooks (hereinafter referred to as "my Trustees") to be Executors and Trustees of this my Will and also to be the trustees hereof for the purposes of the Settled Land Act 1925.

2. I devise my freehold dwellinghouse Sootyacre to my wife Martha during her life so long as she shall remain my widow and during the subsistence of the Settlement hereby created I declare that my wife shall have the power of appointing a new trustee or trustees thereof.
3. Subject thereto I devise my said dwellinghouse to my son Rupert in fee simple.
4. I give devise and bequeath all the rest of my property to my wife absolutely.

> (Duly executed by the Testator and attested).

Now suppose that John Brown dies on March 27, 1972 and his will is proved in the Blacktown District Probate Registry on April 24, 1972. On May 1, 1972 the trustees execute the following Vesting Assent:

By this Assent made the 1st day of May 1972 WE CHARLES BROWN of 4 Gas Street Blacktown and JOSIAH SNOOKS of 11 High Street Blacktown the Executors of John Brown late of Sootyacre Blacktown who died on the 27th day of March 1972 and whose Will dated the 6th day of December 1971 was proved by us in the Blacktown District Probate Registry on the 24th day of April 1972 do as such Personal Representatives Assent to the vesting in Martha Brown of ALL THAT freehold dwellinghouse known as Sootyacre Blacktown for an estate in fee simple.

2. The premises are vested in Martha Brown upon the trusts declared concerning the same by the said Will of the said John Brown.
3. We the said Charles Brown and Josiah Snooks are the trustees of the Settlement for the purposes of the Settled Land Act 1925.
4. The power of appointing a new trustee or new trustees of the Settlement is vested in the said Martha Brown.
5. [Acknowledgment by Trustees of Tenant for Life's right to production of grant of probate of John Brown's will].

> (Duly executed by the Trustees under hand and attested).

Now suppose that Martha makes a will dated April 10, 1972 appointing Josiah Snooks and her son Rupert Brown her executors leaving all her free estate to Rupert Brown. She then dies on December 11, 1972. Josiah Snooks and Rupert Brown, having obtained probate of Martha's will, will then as her general personal representatives make the following Assent:

BY THIS ASSENT dated the 5th day of March 1973 WE JOSIAH SNOOKS of 11 High Street Blacktown and RUPERT BROWN of Flat 4C, Poplar Villas, Blacktown as personal representatives of Martha Brown Assent to the vesting in Rupert Brown of All the property comprised in a Principal Vesting Assent dated the 1st day of May 1972 and known as Sootyacre, Blacktown for an estate in fee simple.
2. [Acknowledgment by the personal representatives of Rupert Brown's right to Probate of the Will of Martha Brown].

(Duly executed by the personal representatives and attested).

Notes

(1) This is an example of a very straightforward and not uncommon chain of events relating to unregistered settled land. The form of the Principal Vesting Assent is based on Form 5, Settled Land Act 1925, First Schedule. A memorandum relating to the Assent will be endorsed on the grant. On the death of the tenant for life the land vests in her general personal representatives, (*Re Bridgett and Hayes Contract* [1928] Ch. 163), the affidavit leading to the grant of probate containing a statement that there was specified settled land but this ceased to be settled on the death of the deceased and that there was no other settled land. Martha's general personal representatives will then vest Sootyacre in Rupert for an estate in fee simple. A memorandum of this Assent will be endorsed on the grant of probate of Martha's will. Section 110(5) of the Settled Land Act 1925 states that where there is an assent relating to land formerly subject to a vesting

instrument which does not state who are the trustees of the settlement for the purposes of the Act, a purchaser of a legal estate is bound to assume that the person in whom the land is vested is entitled free from all limitations charges and powers taking effect under that settlement absolutely and beneficially, and that every statement of fact in the Assent is correct. It will be noted too that the Assent deliberately omits any recital relating to history of the beneficial interests, which lie behind the "curtain."

(2) Were Martha to have remarried, under its terms the settlement would then be at end. It is clear that if the land had remained settled, section 7(4) would have governed the position and Martha would have been bound to convey the settled land to the next tenant for life under the settlement. Equally clearly, had Martha died and the settlement ended naturally, the procedure above would have been followed. The intermediate case, where the settlement ends because Martha forfeits her interest by remarriage is not dealt with clearly by the statute. Ostensibly section 7(5) deals with the position, and this runs:

> "If any person of full age becomes absolutely entitled to the settled land (whether beneficially, or as personal representative, or as trustee for sale, or otherwise) free from all limitations, powers, and charges taking effect under the settlement, he shall be entitled to require the trustees of the settlement, personal representatives, or other persons in whom the settled land is vested, to convey the land to him, and if more persons than one being of full age become so entitled to the settled land they shall be entitled to require such persons as aforesaid to convey the land to them as joint tenants."

However, the legal estate here is not vested in "the trustees of the settlement, personal representatives, or other persons," but is still in Martha, in the same way as it would have been if a further limited owner had been entitled on Martha's remarriage and section 7(4) applicable. It seems, therefore that Rupert should request her to transfer the land to him by ordinary conveyance, and that a deed of discharge would not be necessary (S.L.A. 1925, s. 18(2)(*b*)). A purchaser from Rupert would be entitled to assume that Rupert was absolutely and beneficially entitled by virtue of section 110(5), since the conveyance to Rupert would not state who were the trustees of the settlement for the purposes of the Act.

An equally difficult situation would arise were Martha secretly to remarry and then purport to convey the land as tenant for life to an innocent purchaser. This problem is discussed in the next chapter.

Chapter 5

TRUSTS FOR SALE

Having primarily considered settlements of land governed by the Settled Land Act 1925, it is now necessary to examine settlements by way of trust for sale, which in England are a great deal more common than strict settlements. It has already been pointed out that a trust for sale, (defined as "an immediate binding trust for sale") is excluded from the provisions of the Settled Land Act 1925 and is governed instead by the Law of Property Act 1925 (*ante*, p. 56). The unsuccessful attempts made by the Settled Land Acts 1882-90 to deal with trusts for sale involving a succession of interests have also been mentioned (*ante*, pp. 39-41).

1. Creation

Any person who is in law capable of disposing of property may declare a trust of that property either (a) by a declaration of trust, or (b) in a conveyance of that property, or (c) by will. Since the Statute of Frauds 1677 a declaration of trust respecting any land or interest therein must be evidenced in writing and signed by the person able to declare such trust, or evidenced by inclusion in a will (see now L.P.A. 1925, s. 53(1)(*b*)).

2. Types of trusts for sale

Certain cases exist where land is held on trust for sale by virtue of such a trust being implied by statute. The most commonly met examples are land held in undivided shares (L.P.A. 1925, ss. 34, 35), land held in beneficial joint tenancy (*ibid.* s. 36) and land devolving on personal representatives as a result of an intestacy (Administration of Estates Act 1925,

s. 33). However, none of these instances necessarily involve a *succession* of beneficial interests and so, although the general law relating to trusts for sale applies to them, they will not specifically be considered further. There is in addition the *ad hoc* trust for sale, invented by statute and under which additional equities may be overreached (L.P.A. 1925, s. 2(2)). This will be considered later (*post*, p. 78).

3. Definitions

The "ordinary" trust for sale, as known for many years to conveyancers, must be "an immediate binding trust for sale" if it is to be taken out of the Settled Land Act 1925 (ss. 1(7) and 117(1)(xxx); L.P.A. 1925, s. 205(1)(xxix)). It is of course essential to know which Act does apply to the trusts, since if the Settled Land Act 1925 applies the legal estate will be in the limited or statutory owner, who alone may exercise powers over the land, and if the Law of Property Act 1925 applies the trustees will have the legal estate and exercise the important powers. The word "immediate" may be taken to mean that the operation of the trust for sale must not be postponed to the future. Thus a devise "to A for life with remainder to my trustees upon trust to sell the land and hold the net proceeds thereof upon trust for B absolutely" would not be "immediate." During A's lifetime the land would be settled; on A's death the land would become subject to the trust for sale.

The meaning of "immediate" is usually obvious, though for a case where it was not so obvious see *Re Goodall's Settlement* [1909] 1 Ch. 440 (trust for sale exerciseable at the request of A to whom the rents were meanwhile payable, A having power to terminate the trust; *held*, that the land was settled and A was the tenant for life). The meaning of the word "binding" is more difficult and has given rise to litigation, some of which could have been avoided by more precise statutory drafting (see *e.g. Re Leigh* [1926] Ch. 852). The problem usually arises where it is clear that the land has been settled but it is now questionable whether the settlement has ended. The conclusion from the cases is that to be certain that there is an "immediate binding trust for sale," there must be subsisting no prior interests, legal or equitable, created under a settlement existing at the time of the creation of the trust for sale. Thus where trustees held the legal estate in land on trust to pay two equitable rentcharges, and subject thereto on trust for sale it was held that the trust for sale was not binding (*Re Sharpe's Deed of Release* [1939] Ch. 51; and see *Re Parker's Settled Estates* [1928] Ch. 247 and *Re Norton* [1929] 1 Ch. 84). If the entire legal estate is held by the trustees for sale *as such* (and not, as above, partly as trustees of the annuities) the better opinion is that the trust for sale is "binding" (see *Emmet on Title*, 15th ed. at p. 665).

As always, a "power" to sell must be distinguished from a "trust to sell," but the pre-1926 difficulty of construing a direction "either to retain or sell the land" has been solved by statute which states that the direction is to be construed as a trust for sale with power to postpone the sale (L.P.A. 1925, s. 25(4) applied recently in *Re Edmondson's Will Trusts* [1972] 1 All E.R. 444). Furthermore it is made clear that a trust for sale is an immediate binding trust for sale notwithstanding that it is exerciseable at a person's request or with his consent and notwithstanding a power to postpone sale (L.P.A. 1925, s. 205(1)(xxix)).

4. Duration of trust

It is important for a purchaser of trust land to be sure that the trust for sale on which it is held is still operative. Section 23 of the Law of Property Act 1925 (replacing Conveyancing Act 1911, s. 10(3)) states that where land has become subject to an express or implied trust for sale, such trust shall, so far as regards the safety and protection of any purchaser thereunder, be deemed to be subsisting until the land has been conveyed to or under the direction of the persons interested in the proceeds of sale. It will be noted that this supplies a protection to the purchaser, not the trustees. A trust for sale may also be terminated in other ways, *e.g.* by merger of the beneficial and legal interests in one person, in which case there is no avoiding, on a sale by that person, his bringing the equitable interests on the title (there being no statutory procedure for a declaration by the erstwhile trustees as to the discharge of the trusts, *cf.* S.L.A. 1925, ss. 17(3), 110(5)).

5. Power to postpone

A power to postpone sale is implied by statute in every trust for sale of land unless a contrary intention appears (L.P.A. 1925, s. 25). A contrary intention might comprise a direction by a testator to "sell the land as soon as possible after my death" (*Re Rooke's Will Trusts* [1953] Ch. 716). Section 25(2) indemnifies the trustees against the consequences of exercising their discretion indefinitely and provides that a purchaser of a legal estate shall not be concerned with any directions respecting the postponement of the sale. The flexibility of the trust for sale concept is thus apparent, but it is important to remember that a power to postpone, like other powers given to trustees, must be exercised unanimously. Thus in *Re Mayo* ([1943] Ch. 302) three trustees held land on trust for sale pursuant to section 36 of the Settled Land Act 1925 (which directs that settled land held in undivided shares should be held on statutory trusts for sale as defined in section 36(6)). One trustee wished to sell against the wishes of the other. It was held by Simonds J. that in the absence of mala fides, the "trust for sale will prevail, unless all three trustees agree in exercising the power to postpone" (at p. 304). This is likely to be the case where the trust for sale is by way of settlement, but the court may find a "collateral object" of the trust to preserve the land where it arises by statute owing to co-ownership of the legal estate—*e.g.* where the trust is of the matrimonial home owned by husband and wife (see *per* Devlin L.J. in *Jones* v. *Challenger* [1961] 1 Q.B. 176, 181).

6. Powers pending sale

The difficulties attending the exercise of interim powers of management pending sale by trustees for sale before 1926 have already been discussed (*ante*, p. 41). The position was radically improved by section 28 of the Law of Property Act 1925 (as amended by Law of Property (Amendment) Act 1926, Sched.) which provides that trustees for sale shall have all the powers of a tenant for life and the trustees of a settlement under the Settled Land Act 1925 including those conferred by section 102 of that Act, which include rebuilding houses and improving land. In practice these powers are quite wide enough to allow efficient management of the land, except perhaps with regard to the power of leasing where not infrequently the limitation of the length of occupational leases to fifty years may be too short. This is particularly so where it is desired to sell by way of nominal underlease (for conveyancing convenience) a house held on a lease with more than fifty years unexpired. The trustees could in fact obtain permission from the court under section 57 of the Trustee Act 1925, but the cost of this is rarely worthwhile. (The Trustee Act (Northern Ireland) 1958 neatly surmounts the difficulty by authorising trustees for sale of leasehold land to make a sub-lease of the land or any part of the land with a nominal reversion where this "amounts in substance to a sale and the trustees have satisfied themselves that it is the most appropriate method of disposing of the land" (s. 12(2)).

7. Position of beneficiaries

Although the concept of the trust for sale traditionally presupposes that the land the subject of the trust is investment land rather than land tied to a family, and that it is the trustees who must ordain the fate of land, the beneficiaries of the trust are given the right to request that powers of leasing, accepting surrenders of leases and management until sale be delegated in writing to any beneficiary of full age (not being merely an annuitant) entitled to the rents and profits for life or for any less period. (L.P.A. 1925, ss. 29, 30). Although such powers must be exercised in the names and on behalf of the trustees, the persons to whom the powers are delegated are in the position of trustees as regards their exercise.

The settlement may increase the power of the beneficiaries further in two specific ways. First it is possible (and quite usual) to provide that the trustees' powers may not be exercised without the consent of specified persons (who will normally be or include some or all of the beneficiaries *sui juris*). Although a purchaser is protected provided the consent of any two such persons (being *sui juris*) is obtained, this does not absolve the trustees from obtaining every requisite consent (L.P.A. 1925, s. 26(1) and (2)), with the consent of a parent or guardian sufficing for an infant or receiver for a mental patient (L.P.A. 1925, s. 26(2) and Mental Health Act 1959).

Secondly the settlement may provide that the trustees shall consult the beneficiaries and so far as consistent with the general interest of the trust, give effect to their wishes, or the wishes of a majority, but a purchaser is not concerned to see that this provision has been complied with (L.P.A. 1925, s. 26(3)).

8. Conveyancing

There is no specific conveyancing procedure relating to trusts for sale laid down similar to that in the Settled Land Act 1925. They are in fact often created by means of two instruments. One trust instrument may be a will and on the settlor's death his personal representatives will vest the legal estate in the trustees by written assent. The assent is on the title and the will behind the "curtain." Alternatively a trust instrument may be executed *inter vivos* which declares the trusts, and a conveyance executed contemporaneously vesting the land in the trustees upon the trusts declared by the trust instrument (which remains off the title). However, none of this is strictly necessary. It is quite possible both to declare the trusts and vest the legal estate in the trustees by one document. This is very commonly done, for instance, where a husband and wife buy land jointly. The legislation then provides that "a purchaser of a legal estate from trustees for sale shall not be concerned with the trusts affecting the proceeds of sale" or affecting the land until sale, but as always the purchaser must pay the purchase money to not fewer than two trustees or a trust corporation (L.P.A. 1925, s. 27).

If the title to the land is registered, the trustees for sale (not exceeding four) are registered as proprietors and though it is a general principle that notices of trusts must be excluded from the register (Land Registration Act 1925, s. 74) the beneficiaries interests will be protected provided a restriction is entered on the register (see *ibid*. s. 58(3)) which will be worded to this effect: "No disposition by one proprietor of the land (being the survivor of joint proprietors and not being a trust corporation) under which capital money arises is to be registered except under an Order of the Registrar or of the Court." The capital money will thus be payable to not fewer than two trustees.

9. The effect of a sale

Owing to the doctrine of conversion, from the creation of the trust to sell land the trust assets are regarded as money ("equity looks upon that as done which ought to be done"). It has often been pointed out, therefore, that a sale pursuant to a trust for sale strictly has no "overreaching" effect—interests in land converted to interests in money—since the beneficial interests have been in money since the inception of the trust. The effect of a sale, though, is similar to one under a strict settlement and the beneficiaries' interests are henceforward in the income and capital of pure personalty investments rather than land. The capital money must be paid to not fewer than two trustees and may be invested in the same way as authorised by the Settled Land Act 1925.

A word might be said here as to *"ad hoc"* trusts for sale (*ad hoc* settlements having been mentioned briefly *ante*, p. 59). These have a rather greater overreaching effect than an ordinary conveyance by trustees for sale, though the formalities attending their creation and their rather marginal greater effect has not made them popular devices. Section 2 of the Law of Property Act 1925 deals with the general overreaching effect of conveyances, and subsection (2) (as amended in 1926) states that where a legal estate is subject to a trust for sale and the trustees thereof are either:

(a) two or more individuals approved or appointed by the court, or their successors, or
(b) a trust corporation,

then a conveyance of that legal estate overreaches all equities affecting it (whether or not created prior to the trust for sale) except equities mentioned in subsection (3). These are equitable interests protected by deposit of title deeds relating to the legal estate, restrictive covenants, equitable easements, estate contracts and equitable interests protected by registration (other than annuities, limited owner's charges and general equitable charges, which can, therefore be overreached).

10. A short comparison—strict settlement and trust for sale

Because trusts for sale (a) are much more easily created and the substantive law relating to them better understood by practitioners, and (b) offer, by the device of obtaining consents before sale, a better chance of the land being retained *in specie* if the settlor so desires, trusts for sale are usually chosen as the means of settling land. The better control of sale of the land by this method is paradoxical for the primary trust is, after all, to sell the land. But it is apparently possible, for instance to sell land on trust for sale, the sale to be subject to the consent of (*inter alia*) a contingent remainderman entitled only if the property is unsold at the life tenant's death (compare *Re Inns* [1947] Ch. 576).

On the other hand, full control of the land is in the hands of the life tenant or limited owner under a strict settlement, and it can be strongly argued that it is the beneficiary in possession, not the trustees, who should have the privilege of deciding whether the land should be sold or otherwise dealt with.

A great deal of academic debate has centred around the issue as to whether there should be one code for land settlements, and if so which form that code should take. Examples are the views of Professor M. M. Lewis (in (1938) 54 L.Q.R. 576) who recommends an amendment to the Act to vest the legal estate in the settled land in the settlement trustees, and Professor George Grove in a more modern survey favours a rather similar solution ((1961) 24 M.L.R. 123). Professor Potter favoured a scheme whereby a strict settlement could be created only where there was an intention to do so ((1944) 8 Conv. N.S. 147) and other writers, notably Professors Scamell (in [1957] C.L.P. 152) and *Cheshire* (p. 182) favour the conversion of all settlements into trusts for sale. It is argued later (see Chapter 8) that neither of the present forms is satisfactory as an exclusive code; nevertheless, as the law at present stands, there is no doubt that a trust for sale, if well thought out, provides much the more flexible and satisfactory method of settling land. By a trust for sale, property of all sorts, including pure personalty, may be settled whereas strict settlements are appropriate only to land. Discretionary trusts, too, are more aptly created behind a trust for sale than under a strict settlement necessarily lacking a tenant for life. As a final example, suppose that a testator wishes to provide a residence for his widow but also wishes the residence to be sold on the widow's ceasing to reside there or dying and the capital then to belong absolutely to his son. A settlement made under the Settled Land Act 1925 would have the effect of making the widow the tenant for life. The provision as to a sale of the property on the widow ceasing to reside there is likely to be construed as an illegal restraint on the exercise of the tenant for life's powers under section 106 (see *Re Acklom* [1929] 1 Ch. 195) and a sale of the house by the widow as tenant for life would entitle the widow to the income from the proceeds of sale, which the testator did not intend. Instead, then, the house can be devised to the testator's trustees to be held on trust for sale, with a direction that the trust for sale be postponed so long as the widow should wish to reside in it (rent free) and that her written consent be obtained prior to a sale (compare *Re Herklot's Will Trusts* [1964] 1 W.L.R. 583). Despite the conflict between the purpose of the trust—retention for as long as the widow wished—and the ostensible trust for *sale*, this device more aptly secures the fulfilment of the testator's intentions as is more fully discussed in Chapter 6.

CHAPTER 6

PROBLEMS ARISING ON THE LEGISLATION

THIS chapter is primarily concerned with litigation, much of which arises because of a conflict, or possible conflict, between what the settlor is thought to have intended and what the legislation authorises. Other cases have arisen because of the conceptual contradictions within the legislation itself, the most basic one being the holding out of a limited owner as an owner with powers almost equivalent to those of an absolute owner. Allied to this is the complex framework of checks and balances designed to allow the unfettering of land whilst preventing abuse of power by the tenant for life. In a few cases, it is clear that the legislation throws no light on a potential problem, but since there are no reported cases considering it the answer remains speculative.

1. Is there a settlement?

A preliminary problem sometimes occurs which involves the analysis of a particular limitation to ascertain whether it creates a settlement at all. The cases on this point are mainly concerned with devices designed to give a widow or other beneficiary the right to reside in a particular house for life or a limited period. It should be noted that after 1925 leases for life, or for a term of years determinable on death or marriage of the lessee are converted into terms of ninety years, determinable by proper notice after the event has occurred (L.P.A. 1925, s. 149(6)). Where, therefore, a testator leaves land to his trustee on trust to lease it to his widow for as long as she should be living, on the terms that she could not part with possession of it and in return for a very low rent, which was substantially the position in *Re Catling* ([1931] 2 Ch. 359), it seems that this arrangement should have been regarded as caught by section 149(6) of the Law of Property Act 1925, and the lease one for a term of ninety years. The fee simple should have therefore been vested in the person so entitled subject to the widow's term of years. Instead, in this particular case, the court assumed that a settlement had been created but held, examining the issue which it thought was consequently relevant, that the widow was not a tenant for life or a person having the tenant for life's powers within section 20(i)(iv) of the Settled Land Act 1925, which should be construed as excluding from its ambit tenants for years determinable on life *not holding merely under a lease at a rent*. Had this blind turning not been taken, the device of giving a widow a lease for life at a low rent would have been shown more clearly to be a useful one to adopt in order to avoid the Settled Land Act altogether.

The problem occurs in more direct form where a testator or donor gives land to a beneficiary or trustees subject to another person's right to reside thereon. The right in England is usually expressed as an exclusive one, though it may extend only to part of the donor's land. In Ireland "general rights" to reside in common with others are still quite common. In England this is almost always construed as the grant of a life interest. A few examples will suffice.

In *Re Gibbons* ([1920] 1 Ch. 372) the testator gave to his eldest son "the option of occupying and enjoying the use of" a certain house on the youngest son's coming of age. Similar options were given in succession to other children with an ultimate gift over. The eldest son duly exercised his option and the point concerned the capacity in which he was interested in the house. It was held by the Court of Appeal that the eldest son, on exercising the option, became tenant for life under section 5(2) of the Settled Land Act 1882, though Sterndale M.R. made some play with the difference in wording between a gift authorising a person to "reside" and one, as here, going beyond that by authorising the donee "to occupy and enjoy the use of," a distinction which he called, somewhat enigmatically, "perfectly well known" (at p. 379).

A somewhat similar testamentary gift was before the High

Court in *Re Anderson* ([1920] 1 Ch. 175) where the testator directed that his widow should "be at liberty to use and enjoy" certain residences "for her own personal use and occupation." The main residence was not occupied by the widow on her husband's death and was held by the trustees of the will, with the widow joining in the conveyance to release her right to use the residence according to the terms of the will. Sargant J. held that the testator had conferred on his widow "an option, liberty or licence to occupy personally" but that probably this would have amounted to a life tenancy within the Settled Land Acts had she chosen to avail herself of the option. As she had not, she could not claim any right to the income from the proceeds of sale of the house. The learned judge appeared to think that until the "option" was taken up, the widow had a purely personal right to occupy, the incidents of which, such as a possible right to make short lettings, he did "not consider at all" (at p. 181). The judgment is not a masterpiece of clarity. A more logical analysis of the position would have been to declare the widow to have been entitled to all or nothing, a life tenancy if the "option" was exercised and nothing if it was not. (A possible difficulty in this case might be that the widow might then in either event have been in the position of tenant for life: see Settled Land Act 1882, s. 58(1)(vi).) To condemn the widow to the limbo of having a former personal right to reside solved nothing except the immediate problem before the court.

Two earlier cases are instructive on the English tendency to construe such limitations as settlements without too nice a regard for the interests of persons entitled under the limitation, thus rendering the land a marketable commodity (see the policy statements to this effect in *Bruce* v. *Ailesbury* [1892] A.C. 356; *Re Mundy and Roper's Contract* [1899] 1 Ch. 275). In *Re Carne's Settled Estates* ([1899] 1 Ch. 324) Saint Donat's Castle and grounds, together with six specified fields (being part of the property comprised in the settlement), were vested in trustees upon trust to allow the settlor's widow to occupy them rent free for as long as she might wish to continue to do so. North J. held that this amounted to a gift of an estate for life within the Settled Land Acts. He went on to say (at p. 330):

> "It may be that the mansion-house with the land surrounding it could be sold, and the rest of the settled estate left, with this island the property of someone else in the middle of it. That this would be contrary to the intention of the settlor goes without saying. But the intention of the settlor does not much matter. The question is, what does the Act [*i.e.* the Settled Land Act 1882] say?"

In *Re Baroness Llanover's Will* ([1902] 2 Ch. 679, affirmed by the Court of Appeal [1903] 2 Ch. 16) the testatrix devised certain mansion houses to trustees upon trust to keep up the same and to permit her daughter "at any time and from time to time during her life to reside at said mansion-house, gardens and grounds at Llanover, or at the mansion-house at Great Stanhope Street." Swinfen Eady J. was unable to distinguish the case from *Re Carne's Settled Estates* (*supra*), and that the daughter having "the absolute right of living there" thus had "the powers of a tenant for life within the meaning of the Settled Land Acts." The learned judge added that "it may be that the decision would have surprised the testatrix, and it may be ... that it is not in accordance with her intention; but the Settled Land Act overrides her intention" (at p. 683). See also *Re Duce and Boots Cash Chemist's Contract* [1937] Ch. 642 (trust to permit daughter to use and occupy construed as conferring a life interest); *Re Boyer's Settled Estates* [1916] 2 Ch. 404 (trusts to permit wife and children successively to reside and occupy property conferred life interests within Settled Land Act 1882, s. 58(1)(vi)); *Bannister* v. *Bannister* [1948] 2 All E.R. 133 (oral undertaking by purchaser that vendor might live rent free on property sold for as long as she liked construed as conferring a determinable life interest on the vendor within the Settled Land Act 1925. This case was followed in *Binions* v. *Evans* [1972] 2 W.L.R. 729). As regards registered land, provisions conferring exclusive use of portions of land are briefly discussed in Ruoff and Roper's *Registered Conveyancing* (3rd ed., 1972) at page 245.

With the exception of the rather unsatisfactory decision in *Re Anderson* (*supra*) all the above decisions come down unequivocally in favour of the conferring of life interests upon beneficiaries entitled to occupational rights. There are, however, a handful of cases decided before the passing of the Settled Land Act 1882 which adopt a different approach. Of these the best known is *May* v. *May* ((1881) 44 L.T. 412) where the testator's codicil contained a clause providing: "I also direct that my said wife may reside rent free in my present residence during her life." Fry J. construed this as a licence to live in the house rent free for as long as the widow was so minded, and she therefore had not power to let the house on ceasing to occupy it. In later cases *May* v. *May* tends to be treated as of limited authority since the imposition of the Settled Land Acts, and the policy behind them, obviously were not under consideration by the judge. There is, however, one "rogue" decision which, despite the Settled Land Acts and the authority then extant, construed the familiar provision as something other than a life interest. This was *Re Varley* ((1893) 68 L.T. 665) where the testator's will directed his trustees to allow his wife to reside rent free in his house during widowhood and to have the use, occupation and enjoyment of it. North J. construed this as follows: (at p. 669)

"In my opinion . . . this is not a provision making her a tenant for life or widowhood of the house or enabling her to let it."

Not only is this inconsistent with the mainstream of authorities mentioned above, but the judgment is open to criticism in that it merely states what the interest is not. No clue is provided as to the nature of the interest or what would have happened to the widow's residential right if the person held to be entitled to the estate had let or sold it. (See also *Parker* v. *Parker* (1863) 1 New Rep. 508 (permission to reside in house rent free confers no right to rents and profits thereof); *cf. Coward* v. *Larkman* [1886-90] All E.R. Rep. 896 (testamentary direction that widow should "have the free use and occupation of the house" conferred a life interest therein); *Re Bond* (1904) 4 S.J. 192 (option to reside in any of fourteen houses confers no estate).)

Commonwealth authority also appears to be sparse and of limited value since any importation of the English Settled Land Acts tended to be of an involuntary nature (*e.g.* Nigeria, where the reception of English statutes of general application in force on January 1, 1900 has been held to include them). The Canadian courts in particular have had a handful of cases in which something akin to rights of residence have been in issue and there is some comparatively helpful discussion of the problem in *Moore* v. *Royal Trust Co.* ([1956] 5 D.L.R. 152). There the will directed trustees to permit the testator's son and daughter-in-law "as long as either of them shall occupy the same to have the use and enjoyment of my property [specified] ... and I direct my Trustees that my Trustees shall ... pay the cost of maintaining any building thereon and the insurance of the same against damage by fire." The Supreme Court of Canada held that this conferred no life or other estate but amounted to a personal licence to occupy. Cartwright J. held that continuous occupation was not required but the beneficiaries entitled to the licence were not entitled to let the property or claim any rents or profits from it when not in occupation. The learned judge went on:

> "It is true that on this construction the sale of the properties ... cannot take place during the life time of the beneficiaries unless they consent, and that practical difficulties may be encountered in regard to the trustees renting the properties during such time as the beneficiaries do not wish to avail themselves of the permission to occupy ... and it is hoped that the suggested difficulties will not prove insurmountable."

In the course of construing the gift as conferring, in effect, an irrevocable licence Cartwright J. put his finger accurately on some of the predictable consequential difficulties, though a pious hope is hardly a substitute for a proper solution to the problems.

Some earlier Canadian cases refer to similarly worded gifts and tend to hold that no estate is conferred on the beneficiary, who merely has a "charge" on the land in respect of the occupancy right: see *Wilkinson* v. *Wilson* (1894) 26 O.R. 213; *Condon* v. *Yetman* (1922) 55 N.S.R. 534; see also *Re Marchetti* (1950) 52 W.A.L.R. 20 (Australia). In Scotland, *Wallace* v. *Simmers* (1960 S.C. 225) suggests that the law is similar to that expressed in *Moore* v. *Royal Trust Co.* The Court of Session held that a daughter's right of occupancy was merely a personal right against the grantor and not a real right. It was hence not valid against a successor who bought with notice.

In Ireland, events have taken a different turn. As a result of a number of cases (particularly *National Bank* v. *Keegan* [1931] I.R. 344 and *Kelaghan* v. *Daly* [1913] 2 I.R. 328 analysing the right as a charge in the nature of an annuity and a lien respectively) the legislature has stepped in in both the Republic and Northern Ireland. Statutes now provide that where there is a general right of residence on registered land or an exclusive right of residence in or on part of the land, such right is personal to the person beneficially entitled thereto and is protected by registration as a burden on the land. The land is therefore not settled and the right, despite some contradictory and inadequate judicial decisions, probably amounts to a species of licence, unoverreachable in the sense that a purchaser with notice of it is bound by it (see the Republic's Registration of Title Act 1964, section 81 and Land Registration Act (N.I.) 1970, section 47. The "Irish Right of Residence" is analysed in detail in Northern Ireland Legal Quarterly, Vol. 21, No. 4 (1970) p. 389).

Finally, if *Re Herklot's Will Trusts* ([1964] 1 W.L.R. 583) is indicative, if not directly illustrative, of a safe drafting device in English law, it seems that a right to reside may legitimately and conveniently be created behind a trust for sale, as explained *ante*, p. 81 and discussed *post*, p. 98.

2. Attempts to curtail the powers of the tenant for life

As has already been pointed out, it is a central tenet of the policy of the Settled Land Acts from 1882 onwards that the tenant for life's powers should be unfettered (*ante*, p. 62). The policy of the Act is that no exercise of a power under the Act can cause a forfeiture, or even the divesting of the tenant for life by a determinable limitation over. Section 106 of the 1925 Act achieves this by making (*inter alia*) any provision purporting to forbid or prevent the exercise of these powers, or inducing the tenant for life to abstain from exercising, or putting him in a position inconsistent with the exercise of such power, void. Section 108(2) provides that in the case of a conflict between the provisions of a settlement and of the Act, the Act prevails. Section 109 confirms the validity of additional or larger powers conferred by the settlement.

Two problems in this area have given rise to litigation. The first concerns conditions of residence. An example of this occurred in *Re Acklom* ([1929] 1 Ch. 195) where a testator left his house to Mrs. H. for life with a direction to his trustees that if "and when she shall not wish to reside or continue to reside there" the house should be sold and the proceeds given to charities. During her life tenancy Mrs. H. went abroad for health reasons and owing to illness did not return for about a year. On her return she sold the house under her Settled Land Act powers. Maugham J. held that she was entitled to the income from the proceeds of sale. The charities had argued that Mrs. H. had ceased to reside and had therefore forfeited her interest, prior to the sale. The learned judge, however, found that he had no evidence that at any particular date prior to the sale she had irrevocably decided not only not to continue to reside, but also not to let the house under her powers. "If Mrs. H. was in a position to exercise the powers of a tenant for life (at the date of sale) a provision whereby the proceeds of sale should under the terms of the will pass to the charities is void." Accordingly it was held that she had not forfeited her interest in the proceeds of sale of the leasehold property. However, not all such conditions stipulating residence are *ipso facto* void. If the tenant for life ceases to reside for any reason other than the exercise of his statutory powers, a forfeiture clause will take effect (*Re Haynes* (1887) 37 Ch.D. 306; *Re Trenchard* [1902] 1 Ch. 378).

The second difficulty is where in addition to his life interest the tenant for life is given a conditional right to funds for the upkeep of the land. Thus in *Re Ames* ([1893] 2 Ch. 479) for example, trustees were directed to apply income upon the maintenance of the estate and to pay any surplus to the tenant for life, but if the tenant for life should become disentitled to the possession or income of the settled land, the settled personalty should fall into residue. Clearly the prospect of losing the surplus income was a disincentive to selling the land. The proviso was held void under section 51 of the Settled Land Act 1882, the equivalent of section 106 of the 1925 Act. The tenant for life continued to be entitled to the income from the fund after the sale of the land. But in *Re Aberconway's Settlement Trusts* ([1953] Ch. 647) a majority of the Court of Appeal came to the opposite conclusion. The case concerned Bodnant estate which included Bodnant Hall and gardens. Money was settled for the upkeep of the gardens and horticultural research therein with a gift over of the fund to another settlement if (*inter alia*) the estate and gardens ceased to be enjoyed together. A large part of the gardens were in fact later conveyed to the National Trust. The issue was whether the provision whereunder the upkeep fund should pass to the other settlement was void under section 106. Dankwerts J. held that it was void, so that the income continued to be available for the upkeep of the garden. In reversing this decision the majority of the Court of Appeal were influenced, amongst other things, by the fact that the tenant for life had no "independent" benefit from the fund. The provision putting an end to the trustees' discretionary power to apply the income for the benefit of the gardens was not a deterrent and was not such as to induce the tenant for life not to execute any of his statutory powers. In his dissenting judgment Denning L.J. (as he then was) was influenced by the fact that the tenant for life was faced with two alternative courses of action. He could sell part of the land and lose all the income. Alternatively he could allow part of the gardens to fall into disuse and still be entitled to the whole income. "That seems to me to be the very thing which section 106 was designed to avoid" (at p. 668). The learned judge went on to state that in his view the original trusts should continue with such modification as was necessary to make them apply to the retained part instead of the whole garden.

This particular problem could be solved by making it clear, in an amended version of section 106, that whilst a gift over of income specifically designated for the upkeep of particular land would be valid if all that land were alienated, a gift over, in such circumstances, of income from a personalty fund under which the tenant for life of both land and the personalty fund enjoyed all or part of the personalty fund income for his own use would be void in the same way as any other proviso presently caught by section 106.

3. Limited owner as owner of the fee simple

Under the Settled Land Acts 1882-90, power had to be given to the limited owner to convey more than could possibly be vested in him, namely the whole legal estate in the land. (This would either have been vested in trustees, or split up between the beneficiaries, see ante, p. 38). There is nothing particularly inelegant in this concept and, indeed, a mortgage by demise of freeholds is to this day given a similar power to sell the fee simple estate of the mortgagor (L.P.A. 1925, s. 88). In 1925, as has been explained in Chapter 3, it was a central plank of the new policy to invest the limited owner with the full fee simple absolute in possession, or term of years if the settled land was leasehold. Having thus transformed him ostensibly into a full beneficial owner, the powers given to the limited owner are laid down specifically, and in some respects in a severely curtailed form. Furthermore the whole conveyancing *trompe l'oeil* depends for its efficacy on statutory provisions which only apply if the limited owner is *in fact* the limited owner in possession. The purchaser is usually forbidden by the terms of the "certificate" scheme to investigate the trusts which lie behind the curtain. The scheme contains too many contradictory concepts to produce problem-free conveyancing, as the following examples show.

(a) Absence of power

There are two possible fundamental problems here. One is where a person who is in fact merely a limited owner purports to deal with the land (*e.g.* by fraudulently suppressing deeds) as absolute owner. An example of this occurred in *Weston* v. *Henshaw* ([1950] Ch. 510). Argument in the case involved three sections in particular of the Settled Land Act 1925. Section 18(1)(*a*) lays down the basic proposition that any disposition by the tenant for life unauthorised by the Act or other statute or the vesting instrument (in the case of larger powers) is void as regards the legal estate. Section 112(2) states that references to "sale, purchase, exchange, mortgaging, charging, leasing, or other disposition or dealing" are to be construed as extending to sales and other transactions "*under this Act*." Section 110(1) states that on a sale or other disposition, a purchaser dealing in good faith with a tenant for life shall, as against all parties entitled under the settlement, "be conclusively taken to have ... complied with all the requisitions of this Act."

The facts in *Weston* v. *Henshaw* (*supra*) were that land was sold by a father to his son in 1921. In 1927 the son sold it back to his father. His father then settled the land by will, the material limitations being to the son for life with remainder to a grandson contingently on attaining the age of twenty-five. On the son's becoming entitled to his life interest a vesting deed was executed in his favour under the Act and the deeds relating to the property handed to him. The son then mortgaged the property to the defendant, representing that he was seised in fee simple. The son concealed the existence of the settlement by suppressing all deeds later than the original conveyance to him by his father in 1921. The grandson, who was on the son's death absolutely entitled to the property, sued for a declaration that the mortgages were void. The argument for the plaintiff grandson was that since (a) the son who had charged the property was in fact a tenant for life, and (b) the mortgage was not for a purpose permitted for raising money under section 71 of the Act, the charge was void and did not create any legal interest in the defendant. The defendant, in arguing that the mortgage was valid, relied on reading section 18(1)(a) in conjunction with section 112(2), so that although the unauthorised disposition was apparently void under section 18(1)(a), that provision was subject to the limitation that it applies only to a disposition made, or purporting to be made, by a tenant for life as such. Dankwerts J., however, rejected this ingenious argument on the ground that it would make nonsense of section 18 to limit it to transactions under the Act, "because it is essentially concerned with transactions which are not in pursuance of the Act and which it therefore makes void." Nor, the learned judge decided did section 110(1) avail the defendant since the section only applies "to a person who is dealing with the tenant for life or statutory owner as such, whom he knows to be a limited owner, and with regard to whom he might be under a duty." The result was that the charge was void, unfortunate though this was for the innocent defendant.

Two features of this happily unusual situation might be noticed especially. First, there is some irony in the fact that the recital in the mortgage as to the mortgagor-tenant for life being seised in fee simple was correct. Secondly, since the mortgagee-defendant purchased a legal estate without notice of the equities affecting it, as a matter of basic principle he ought to have taken free from those equities. (This case indicates what is apparently the sole exception to this rule. This basic principle was reaffirmed recently in *Caunce* v. *Caunce* ([1969] 1 W.L.R. 286) where a legal mortgagee of a husband's legal estate without notice of his wife's beneficial interest in an undivided half-share was held to take priority to the wife's beneficial interest. A wife with such an equitable interest is now able to protect her interest by registration under the Matrimonial Homes Act 1967—see Matrimonial Proceedings and Property Act 1970, s. 38).

In fact the Act contains a useful, and little noticed, direction to the trustees which could if observed, avoid the main dangers of the tenant for life passing himself off as absolute owner by suppression of the vesting deed, particularly if he settles the land on himself for life. Section 98(3) directs the trustees of the settlement to "require that notice of the last or only principal vesting instrument be written on one of the documents under which the tenant for life acquired his title" where "if the settlement were not disclosed, it would appear that the tenant for life ... was absolutely and beneficially entitled to the settled land." But this would not avail a purchaser who deliberately refrained from enquiring as to the tenant for life's title. Previously it was thought unlikely that such a person could be said to deal "in good faith" under section 110(1) (see *Gilmore* v. *The O'Connor Don* [1947] I.R. 462 (Irish Sup. Ct.) and dicta in *Davies* v. *Hall* [1954] 1 W.L.R. 855). But the decision of Ungoed-Thomas J. in *Re Morgan's Lease* ([1972] Ch. 1) would, if correct, undermine the basis of such cases as *Weston* v. *Henshaw* in so far as they were based on a purchaser's *knowing* that he was dealing with a tenant for life. There, a purchaser-lessee who took an option for a lease from a person whom he believed to be the absolute owner, but who was actually a tenant for life, was nevertheless held protected by section 110(1), and the option was therefore deemed to have been properly granted under the provisions of the Settled Land Act 1925 to him as a bona fide purchaser. (See also generally Maudsley in (1973) 36 M.L.R. 25.) Too much cannot be read into this case, however, since it seems that the granting of the option would in any event have been within the tenant for life's powers under section 51 of the Act.

A second fundamental problem arises where a disposition is made by a person purporting to be tenant for life but who has in fact ceased to be so. An example would be where land is settled by will on the testator's wife for life or until remarriage with remainder to his son in fee simple. The testator's widow then does remarry secretly, but purports to dispose of the settled property, which by this time should have been conveyed to the remainderman. The purchaser, however, takes in good faith on the basis of the vesting assent in favour of the widow, and the trustees accept the capital money in ignorance of the remarriage. The purchaser, being unable to inspect the trust instrument, is probably unaware that there is such a limitation over. It seems that in this case the purchaser would obtain the legal estate, since this would have still been vested in the erstwhile tenant for life, but since the widow is not *in fact* the tenant for life she would lack the statutory power to overreach the equitable interests. The purchaser has constructive notice from the vesting assent of the beneficial interests created by the trust which therefore continue to be attached to the purchaser's legal estate. Section 110(2) would not avail the purchaser since he was not buying "a legal estate in settled land" and would not be entitled to make the assumptions contained in that section which would have ordinarily protected him. Were the statutory provision to refer to a purchaser of a legal estate in settled land or of land which, on the basis of the instrument vesting the land in the vendor, he genuinely believed to be settled, the result would be more satisfactory (see *Megarry and Wade*, p. 315). It is interesting to note that this situation could not arise in this way under the pre-1926 law, since the purchaser would inspect the trust instrument and would be put on enquiry as to the widow's remarriage.

(b) Abuse of power

This involves the reverse side of the coin. Since under the statutory scheme the entire legal estate and a number of important powers are vested in the limited owner, it is essential that protection against abuse of power is given by the scheme. Section 53 of the 1882 Act and section 107 of the 1925 Act enjoin the tenant for life to "have regard to the interests of all parties entitled under the settlement, and [he] shall, in relation to the exercise thereof by him, be deemed to be in the position and to have the duties and liabilities of a trustee for those parties" (*ante*, p. 34). It will have been seen that the cases on these sections, such as *Wheelwright* v. *Walker* ((1883) 23 Ch.D. 752) suggest that it is the trustees' duty to intervene to restrain a dealing "if a tenant for life attempted to commit what may be called a fraud, and proposed to sell the property for something below its real value...." (*per* Pearson J. at page 762, and in this connection see *Wheelwright* v. *Walker* ((1883) 31 W.R. 912) where, in later proceedings, the tenant for life, proposing to sell at a price below that offered by a remainderman, was restrained from selling otherwise than by public auction unless the offer was first communicated to the remainderman). In fact section 42 of the 1882 Act and section 97 of the 1925 Act explicitly exempt the trustees from liability "for not making, bringing, taking or doing any such application, action, proceeding or thing, as they might, bring, take or do." Nevertheless, Pearson J.'s judgment is useful in indicating when intervention would be proper, even if there is no "duty" to do so. It was also made clear soon after the 1882 Act was passed that a dealing which was otherwise proper could not be invalidated if the tenant for life "is selling out of ill will or caprice, or because he does not like the remainderman, because he desires to be relieved from the trouble of attending to the management of land, or from any other such object, or with any such motive" (*per* Chitty J. in *Cardigan* v. *Curzon-Howe* (1885) 30 Ch.D. 531, 540). There is, then, a divergence between the nature of the trusteeship imposed on the tenant for life as interpreted by the cases, and the more stringent duties imposed upon ordinary trustees. But the comparative paucity of litigation on the point, particularly since 1925, indicates that the problem is largely theoretical.

The other devices used to prevent abuse of power to the prejudice of the beneficiaries are the necessity of giving notice prior to the exercise of the more important powers, exceptionally the necessity of obtaining the trustees' consent thereto and, as a safeguard against fraud, the necessity of paying capital money to the trustees or into court (see *ante*, pp. 62, 66). Further if the tenant for life wishes to buy the settled land himself he may do so if the trustees exercise his powers under section 68 (see *ante*, p. 65). In both these respects the legislation appears to have been satisfactory.

(c) *Refusal to exercise powers*

The potential problem here has been neatly surmounted by the legislation (which gives power to any person interested to apply to the court, see *ante*, p. 66), but section 24 only applies where the court is satisfied that the tenant for life has ceased to have a substantial interest in the settled land "by reason of bankruptcy, assignment, incumbrance, or otherwise." The Act does not tackle the more central problem of the tenant for life who unreasonably refuses to exercise his powers, thus failing to prevent the decay of the settled land, or to exploit an opportunity of development, and who continues to have a substantial interest in the land. This would be less serious if there were an obligation on the tenant for life under the general law to keep the property in repair. But it was held in *Re Cartwright* ((1889) 41 Ch.D. 532) that a tenant for life who is impeachable for waste is not liable for *permissive* waste, unless the settlement imposes on him the obligation to repair (*Woodhouse* v. *Walker* (1880) 5 Q.B.D. 404). Underhill drew attention to this problem in his lecture on the Law of Settled Land in 1901 (see *A Century of Law Reform*, at pp. 296-97). He said: "Either the life tenant ought to be made to keep property in repair, or the Court ought to have jurisdiction in every case to sanction a charge for the purpose on the inheritance. Something ought to be done to clear away an *impasse* which is a disgrace to our law." Once again, the cause of the problem lies in the fact that the limited owner is given almost complete dominion over land in which his own personal interest is in the occupation or income for life or other limited period.

4. Problems as to trusts for sale

The initial problem here is whether there is an "immediate binding trust for sale" or whether the trust for sale is not such as to take the settlement out of the Settled Land Act. This has been discussed in Chapter 5 and all that remains to be said is well said in a recent report in Northern Ireland on Registration of Title to Land (Cmd. 512): "The dual system in England appears to have given rise to some very wasteful litigation in which the issue was whether a particular arrangement was a settlement under which the disposition powers resided in the tenant for life, or a trust for sale with the powers being in the trustees, there being no doubt at all that *someone* had the necessary power" (para. 141).

(a) *Conflict between the trust to sell and the idea of a settlement*

We have already seen that the trust for sale has proved itself both a simpler and more flexible method of settling land (see *ante,* Chapter 5). Nevertheless there is a conflict between the primary trust to sell and the intention of the settlor in such cases where the settlor wishes the land to be retained and drafts the trust accordingly.

This basic conflict arose in unmistakable form in *Re Herklot's Will Trusts* ([1964] 1 W.L.R. 583). The material provisions in the will under consideration ran: "4. I give the residue of my property to my trustees upon trust to sell and call in the same with power to postpone such sale and calling in indefinitely without being responsible for loss ... 6. My trustees shall pay the income of the said moneys to the said A ... F ... G ... during her life without prejudice to the trust for sale herein contained and shall permit her to reside in my house No. 8, Cannon Place, aforesaid during her life for so long as she wishes she paying all outgoings insurances and repairs in respect thereof." There then followed a disposal of the property, subject to the life interest, which, as varied by codicil, had the effect of entitling the plaintiff to either one third of the trust fund (*i.e.* the unsold property and the investments representing the sold property) or to the house *in specie* "absolutely if he desires it." Ungoed-Thomas J. analysed the question as being "whether, on the construction of this will, the testatrix takes out of the trust for sale which she has declared, the house which was the subject of the gift in this case." The learned judge held (1) that the testatrix did not intend to take the house out of the trust for sale, and (2) that the provision entitling the life tenant to reside in the house was akin to saying that the house must not be sold without her consent, and this was in no way inconsistent with the statutory definition of a trust for sale in the Law of Property Act 1925, and (3) having regard to the fact that it was implicit that there should be no sale in the lifetime of the plaintiff-remainderman, the plaintiff's consent to the sale was also a pre-requisite. The result was, then, that the will was held to impose an immediate binding trust for sale exercisable only with the consent of the life tenant and the remainderman, a convenient and sensible solution, but not one readily perceptible from the actual wording of the will. As a commentator pointed out, "this decision should ... be treated with care, for in other cases the gift of property to provide a residence for a beneficiary has been held to create settled land (see 28 Conv. (N.S.) 312-13, and on rights of residence generally see *ante*, pp. 82-88).

The lessons to be learnt from this case seem to be: (1) If it is desired to give a specific beneficiary a right to reside in a house but not to create settled land, it is possible to do this behind a trust for sale exercisable on the consent of the beneficiary or beneficiaries interested in the retention or sale of the land—a position which the drafting of the will in *Re Herklot's Will Trusts* failed safely to achieve; (2) sympathy is not undue for a lay testator who is told that the above device involves a primary *trust* to sell, rather than a power to do so when agreed and convenient, and that the only alternative is a settlement governed by the Settled Land Act 1925 which would give the life tenant an *unrestricted* power to sell.

The imposition of a statutory trust for sale in cases of co-ownership, though not necessarily entailing a succession of interests, also underlines the practical difficulty of reconciling the duty imposed by the trust with what may be its collateral purpose—*e.g.* retention of a jointly owned matrimonial home. It is clear from *Jones* v. *Challenger* ([1961] 1 Q.B. 176) that the court is in certain circumstances prepared to recognise this collateral object since not to do so would be "something akin to mala fides" (*per* Devlin L.J.). In cases where the marriage has broken down the court has tended to hold that the collateral purpose, namely use as a matrimonial home, has disappeared, and has thus ordered a sale on the initiative of one of the owner-spouses (see *e.g. Jones* v. *Challenger, supra*, and *Rawlings* v. *Rawlings* [1964] 2 All E.R. 804). When it is a deserted wife who is the co-owner and she is forced to sell the erstwhile matrimonial home by virtue of the primary trust for sale and the rationale in the above two cases, difficult questions of doing justice as between the parties may arise—a sale may make the wife homeless and a refusal to sell may deprive the husband of any benefit from his investment. Once this stage is reached it is immaterial whether a flexible trust or a power is involved. The problem becomes one of family security and basic economics.

(b) May the powers of trustees for sale be restricted?

Although there has been some litigation over the years on whether an apparent trust for sale is an "immediate binding trust for sale," there has been little direct consideration of the implications of section 28(1) of the Law of Property Act 1925. This gives to trustees for sale "all the powers of a tenant for life and the trustees of a settlement under the Settled Land Act 1925, including in relation to the land the powers of management conferred by that Act during a minority."

Take as an example the lay testator who wishes his house to be sold after his death and the proceeds to be invested. When informed by his solicitor that a power to postpone will be implied unless a contrary intention is expressed ((L.P.A. 1925, s. 25) though such a power is in practice almost invariably expressly inserted) he accepts this. He is, however, disturbed when informed that pending sale the trustees have power to lease the land for occupational purposes for up to fifty years (see S.L.A. 1925, s. 41). He points out that he desires a trust for *sale*, the sale being postponed to a time when the best bargain may be struck and otherwise convenient, and this is inconsistent with the trust to sell. He therefore wishes to negative the trustees leasing powers, except, perhaps, on a very short-term basis. Can he do so?

The answer is generally assumed to be negative. Special provision is made for the trust for sale itself to be exercisable subject to consents, and as has been seen (*ante*, p.79) this consent may be unlikely to be forthcoming. Further, the power to postpone expressly may be negatived. Otherwise the powers of trustees for sale are assumed to be as indefeasible as all the powers of a tenant for life under section 106 of the Settled Land Act 1925. The problem was mooted by counsel in the rather unsatisfactory case of *Re Davies* ([1932] 1 Ch. 530) but the tentative judgment of Maugham J. does not clearly solve it. The learned judge did indeed state that if there were a sale or a lease under the statutory trusts the provision in the will which put an end to a beneficiary's interest were he to cease to reside on a certain farm must be deemed to be void, but the decision seems to have been based on the extent of the "powers and provisions" mentioned in section 35 of the Law of Property Act 1925 (definition of the "statutory trusts") rather than section 28. It also points to another difficulty, namely that under a trust for sale it may not be the trustee's own beneficial interest which is threatened by a forfeiture clause in the settlement (for the trustee may not have one). It is more likely that a beneficiary without any power to deal with the land would be the victim of such a clause. In this event it seems that the wording of section 106 of the Settled Land Act 1925 is inappropriate to meet the problem, since such a clause could not be said to inhibit *the beneficiary* from dealing with the land; he has no power to do so.

CHAPTER 7

TAXATION AND THE MODERN SETTLEMENT

1. INTRODUCTION

This chapter is concerned with modern settlements of land, and in particular seeks to summarise how fiscal considerations have to a large extent dominated the form of the settlement. The extent of the impact of taxation on land-owners has been detailed in Chapter 1. It only remains to remind the reader that there is nothing new about the proposition that the form of a settlement must be dictated by the incidence of taxation. As soon as the Court of Chancery recognised the interest of a *cestui que use* a ready means was found to exist of evading the feudal burdens which fell on the death of a tenant solely *seised* of land. Then began the familiar game of cat and mouse between legislature and subject, culminating, but by no means terminating, in the Statute of Uses of 1535.

Something, too, might be said about tax avoidance. The following general points should be borne in mind:

(1) Taxation is the creature of statute and the judges in interpreting the statute will do so strictly. If there is doubt as to the scope of a charging section, the taxpayer should be given the benefit of the doubt. In practice, important loopholes revealed by enterprising litigants tend to be closed by the legislature in the next following Finance Act.

(2) Despite some recent knocks, the doctrine propounded by the House of Lords in *I.R.C.* v. *Duke of Westminster* ([1936] A.C. 1) that the court may not go behind the form with which a document is clothed and discover a "substance" less (or more) favourable to the taxpayer still applies (but see comment in [1969] B.T.R. 256 on *I.R.C.* v. *Land Securities Investment Trust Ltd.* [1969] 1 W.L.R. 604).

102

(3) Besides containing "loopholes," fiscal legislation contains specific exemptions from the charge to tax, and also provisions which may legitimately be described as "tax traps" in that a person may, by undertaking a transaction in a certain way, and without intention to avoid tax, find himself paying a preternaturally large amount of tax, quite possibly because the provision is framed very widely to counteract tax avoidance. Section 451 of the Income and Corporation Taxes Act 1970, for instance (dealing with payments by trustees to the settlor) has been described by Lord Reid in *I.R.C.* v. *Bates* ([1968] A.C. 483) as "so widely drawn as to be a trap for the innocent" (p. 504) and the result of "thoroughly bad draftsmanship" (p. 507). As far as the specific exemptions are concerned, parliament's intention is presumed to be to benefit the taxpayer if he orders his affairs in a certain way. An important example in the field of settlements is the exemption from estate duty of property settled by one spouse on the other on the death of the second spouse provided the second spouse was not competent to dispose of the property and it was dutiable on the death of the first spouse (Finance Act 1894, s. 5(2) as amended).

(4) The professional adviser who fails adequately to consider both exemptions and "tax-traps" is liable to be sued for negligence. In most cases, provided "avoidance" rather than dishonest "evasion" is involved, morality is no more in issue than where a lawyer is defending a person charged, perhaps rightly, with a criminal offence. The lawyer operates within the bounds of the law laid down by judges and parliament, and freely changeable by the latter at regular intervals. His informed guidance must be made available to his clients in the same way as in any other profession. (It is sometimes salutary to remember the reproach of Holy Writ: "Woe unto you, lawyers! for ye have taken away the key of knowledge".)

It is proposed first to consider the main relevant taxing provisions and then to assess their more detailed effect on the form of a settlement of land. It must be borne in mind, though, that the taxation of gifts and settlements, whether of land or pure personalty, is a complex topic and a detailed examination of the law is beyond the scope of this book. The summary of the taxes which follows is intended as a very elementary introduction for readers who have not before formally studied tax, or to refresh the memory of those who have, and should help to clarify the explanation of the applicability of these taxes to settlements. When settlements are drafted in practice, tax counsel's opinion is often sought before the draft is finalised.

2. THE TAXES APPLICABLE TO SETTLEMENTS GENERALLY

The following is a summary of the effect of the main taxes which have to be considered when dealing with settlements involving a succession of interests:

(1) Capital gains tax

This is levied at a flat rate of 30 per cent. on the chargeable gains of the year of assessment, less allowable losses. The rate may be less than 30 per cent. for individuals (not trustees) who take advantage of the "half-income" rule—*i.e.* where the gain does not exceed £5,000, half the gain may be added to the taxpayer's income and charged to income tax as the top slice thereof. The tax is imposed on the disposal of chargeable assets, including by way of gift and settlement whether or not the settlor retains a legal or equitable interest, and its working is best illustrated by example. Suppose X disposes of a plot of land at a profit, X not being a trader in land. The computation is based on the *net* gain accruing to him, *i.e.* his disposal price less his acquisition price and all other overheads thus:

Sale proceeds		£10,000
Less Cost	£6,000	
Advertising	10	
Agents charges	50	
Transfer charges and stamp duty	50	

Legal charges on pur-chase and sale	155	£6,265
Chargeable gain		£3,735

There are special rules to prevent retrospective effect where the chargeable asset was held on April 6, 1965 (*i.e.* acquired before April 7, 1965). The law is contained in the Finance Act 1965 as frequently amended since.

During the currency of a settlement there may be further liability to capital gains tax, on disposals of trust property by the trustees or deemed disposals by the trustees such as where a beneficiary becomes absolutely entitled as against the trustee to trust assets (F.A. 1965, s. 25(31).

Death is no longer an occasion as a result of which there is a charge to capital gains tax, this tax and estate duty being in principle mutually exclusive. Personal representatives (or trustees where the interest is settled) are deemed to have acquired the relevant property at market value at death, but since no tax is exigible, this often results in a "free uplift" of the bare value of the property.

Section 29 of the Finance Act 1965 contains an important and well-known exemption from capital gains tax in favour of an individual's only or main residence. This exemption extends to gains accruing to trustees on the disposal of a house if during the period of ownership the house has been occupied as the only or main residence of a person entitled to occupy it under the terms of a settlement (s. 29(9)). By concession, this relief is extended to a beneficiary entitled to the whole income from the residence or from its sale who is permitted by the trustees to occupy it (extra-statutory concession D.3 in Board of Inland Revenue's Booklet I.R.I.). It will thus be seen that the exemption in favour of private dwelling-houses contained in section 29 extends to those occupied by beneficiaries under strict settlements or trusts for sale in the above circumstances.

(2) Estate duty

This is a tax levied under the Finance Act 1894, as amended, on property passing on death. As with income tax the system is progressive, *i.e.* the greater the taxable amount the higher the percentage of tax. In a simple case it is necessary merely to aggregate the deceased's total assets (including gifts made before death which are caught under the legislation), deduct from the total the deceased's debts and pay duty on the balance according to the following scale (as from 1972):

Slice of net capital value		Rate per cent	Cumulative
Exceeding £	Not Exceeding £	of duty	duty
15,000	20,000	25	1,250
20,000	30,000	30	4,250
30,000	40,000	35	7,750
40,000	50,000	40	11,750
50,000	60,000	45	16,250
60,000	80,000	50	26,250
80,000	100,000	55	37,250
100,000	150,000	60	67,250
150,000	200,000	65	99,750
200,000	500,000	70	309,750
Over 500,000		75	

Duty is charged under section 1 of the 1894 Act in the way more precisely defined in section 2. The following is a summary of the charging provisions of section 2, all of which could possibly be relevant when considering settlements:

S. 2(1)(*a*)—catches property of which the deceased was at the time of his death competent to dispose—*i.e.* all the deceased's "free estate," or absolutely owned property, a severable share under a joint tenancy or an undivided share, property disposable under a general power of appointment, and certain other assets.

S. 2(1)(b)—catches interests in settled property passing on death, including on the cesser of a life interest, or on the death of a beneficiary under a discretionary settlement to the extent that the beneficiary has benefitted under the settlement within the material period. In the case of the cesser of a straightforward life interest the charge to duty extends to the *whole* capital of the settled property. It also applies where a power or trust for accumulation terminates on the settlor's death.

S. 2(1)(c)—catches gifts, whether absolute or by way of settlement, whenever made by the deceased unless made more than seven years before death (four in Northern Ireland) to the entire exclusion of the donor.

S. 2(1)(d)—formerly caught some annuities or other interests arising on death, but repealed by Finance Act 1969.

S. 2(1)(e)—catches deceased's interest under a partnership passing on his death to continuing partners.

S. 2(1)(f)—catches property subject to certain options exercisable by reference to the deceased's death.

S. 2(1)(g)—catches property in Scotland which in England would have passed as settled property under section 2(1)(b).

In addition to the charging provisions above, there is one other important charging provision contained in the Finance Act 1940, the effect of which is to charge the assets of a company formerly controlled by the deceased to the extent that he has received income therefrom in excess of reasonable remuneration for services. It is also important to note that where property is caught by more than one charging provision, duty is not exigible twice (F.A. 1894, s. 7(10)).

There are a number of exemptions and reliefs from duty, some of which are of great importance when planning settlements. They are discussed later.

(3) Stamp duty

Stamp duty is a duty on documents, imposed at rates which vary by reference to how the document is classified. A document not duly stamped may not be given in evidence, except in criminal proceedings (Stamp Act 1891, s. 14(4)). Voluntary dispositions evidenced by a deed (such as a conveyance to trustees) are liable to conveyance or transfer duty at the *ad valorem* rate of 1 per cent assessed on the adjudicated value of settled property. In the case of land it is important to note that if a certificate is inserted in the deed stating that the transaction is not part of a larger transaction or a series of transactions and the value does not exceed £10,000, no duty is payable; if the value is over £10,000 but not in excess of £15,000 the duty is at half the full rate, namely $\frac{1}{2}$ per cent (F.A. 1972).

(4) Income tax

It must be borne in mind that a settlement of land may well be a device for securing income to beneficiaries, for example by the renting out of property held upon trust for sale or of all or part of property held under a strict settlement. In this respect the rules are applicable to the income arising under these settlements in the same way as for the personalty settlements. It is also important to appreciate that in a highly progressive tax system, if a wealthy man can successfully hive off the top slice of his income to a person not taxable at the higher rates, either by a simple settlement by way of covenant to pay the income for a period which can exceed six years (see I.C.T.A. 1970, s. 434) or by a transfer of the capital yielding that slice of income, a substantial tax saving is incurred. If it were possible to benefit by this device persons to whom he owed an obligation to support, for instance his children, the overall economic effect is even more dramatic. In order to avoid abuse of this system, a number of rules exist which the settlement must observe. If it fails to do so, their effect is to make the transfer of income nugatory for tax purposes.

The treatment for income tax purposes of income arising under a settlement is extremely complex in application. The following is merely an outline of the position where income arises (*e.g.* rents from land) and is payable to and ultimately distributable by trustees.

(a) *Trustees* are liable to pay tax on trust income at the "basic rate" as from 1973-74, the basic rate having at present been fixed at 30 per cent (F.A. 1971, s. 39). Trustees are not entitled to claim personal reliefs, nor are they assessable to the higher rates of tax (formerly surtax) however much income they receive in one year of assessment if the income is distributed. As from 1973, if the income is or may be accumulated, it will all attract the investment income surcharge of an additional 15 per cent. (Budget Statement 1973). Income from land will usually be received gross under Schedule A by the trustees, but income from securities will normally already have had tax deducted at source.

(b) *The beneficiary's* tax position varies according to whether or not he has a vested right to the income. If he has, he is taxed whether or not he actually received the income (*Hamilton-Russell's Executors* v. *I.R.C.* ((1943) 25 T.C. 200 (C.A.)). If, having only a discretionary or contingent interest, the income is accumulated and not applied for his benefit, he cannot be assessed thereon. Conversely, if income to which he is not *entitled* is paid to him pursuant to the exercise of the trustees' discretion, he will be assessable on the amount so paid. In this case he will receive the income less the tax deducted by the trustees at the appropriate rate and thereafter it will depend upon the level of his total income from all sources whether he will be able to reclaim the tax deducted (using his own personal reliefs) or will be assessable at a higher rate. Particular care must be taken when considering whether to make up a beneficiary's income out of capital, for such a payment is likely to be assessed as income in the beneficiary's hands (see *Cunard's Trustees* v. *I.R.C.* ([1946] 1 All E.R. 159), payments out of capital to life tenant of house to enable her to live in her customary degree of comfort pursuant to power in the will assessed as income).

(c) As regards *the settlor*, if the settlement is fully effective the capital and the income arising from it should both have been fully alienated leaving no residual tax liability. However, as explained above, a number of complex anti-avoidance provisions exist in the Income and Corporation Taxes Act 1970 which can make the transfer of income ineffective. These are the main ones:

(i) If the settlement income is paid to or for the benefit of the settlor's unmarried child, the income is deemed to be the income of the settlor if the child is under eighteen years of age (s. 437 as amended). Reciprocal arrangement under which settlors benefit each others' children are caught, but the provision applies to a "child" not a grandchild, of the settlor. The only effective way of settling capital on the settlor's own children is by way of an irrevocable settlement under which the income is accumulated; any income *distributed* to the children will be caught and added back to the settlor's income (ss. 437-38). A settlement is not "irrevocable" if, *inter alia*, any person has power to revoke the settlement so that the settlor or his spouse benefits from the settled property (s. 446).

(ii) If the income under a settlement is accumulated, the income so accumulated is treated as that of the settlor if the capital or income can become applicable to the settlor or his spouse (*i.e.* the settlor retains an interest under the settlement) *except* on the happening of certain specified events (s. 447). These specified events include the bankruptcy of some person who is or may become beneficially entitled to the income or property, or the assigning or charging of this interest and the death under the age of twenty-five or some lower age who would be beneficially entitled to that income or property on attaining that age (s. 447(2)). Furthermore, the accumulated income is treated as that of the settlor to the extent that capital sums (including loans) are paid by the trustees to the settlor or his spouse (s. 448).

To summarise, the only safe course is for the settlement to exclude from all benefit the settlor or his spouse, except on failure of the trusts under the provisions of section 447, or if the entitlement to the benefit only accrues to the settlor's spouse after his (or her) death (*Vestey's Executors* v. *I.R.C.* ([1949] 1 All E.R. 1108 (H.L.)) because the term "wife" does not include "widow." It is also inadvisable, though not necessarily disastrous, for the settlor or his spouse to be a trustee, particularly if the settlement includes shares in a family company which, if added to his beneficial holding, would give the settlor a controlling interest (see *Barclay's Bank Ltd.* v. *I.R.C.* [1961] A.C. 509). Sums advanced under the terms of the settlement to the settlor's relatives might also be regarded as gifts vulnerable on the settlor's death within seven years (see F.A. 1940, s. 44 as amended). So, too, the existence of a charging clause which any well-drawn settlement should include might presently or in the future benefit a professional settlor or his spouse, so affecting the "revocability" of the settlement. In order to avoid these and other possible snags, the safest course is to retain to the settlor the right to appoint new trustees *other than himself* during his lifetime.

Finally, an attempt should be made to assess the advantages of accumulating income in the light of the Budget Statement 1973. As mentioned above, since all income so accumulated is to be taxable at a total of 45 per cent. (basic rate of 30 per cent. plus surcharge of 15 per cent.) this no longer constitutes an attractive proposition in many cases. Where such income is in fact distributed, the beneficiaries will have a possible repayment claim as to the full 45 per cent., but such distribution is inconsistent with the idea of accumulating income so that it is receivable eventually as an accretion to capital (and subject at the most to capital gains tax) at a later date by the beneficiaries. The 45 per cent. rate is considerably more penal than the standard rate of 38.75 per cent. applicable to such income in the tax year 1972-73. It should further be remembered that property the income of which is accumulated for a period terminating on the deceased's death is caught for estate duty by the Finance Act 1894, s. 2(1)(*b*). If an accumulating settlement is made, an alternative period of accumulation as permitted by the Law of Property Act 1925, s. 164-166 (as amended by the Perpetuities and Accumulations Act 1964) should be chosen—for example, twenty-one years from the settlor's death. Clearly the present fiscal attack on accumulated income (which paradoxically seems to implement the measures threatened but not imposed by a

Chancellor of the former Government—see (1968) 761 H. C. Deb. 293) signifies that income should be accumulated in future with great discretion.

3. TAX AND THE SETTLEMENT OF LAND

It is necessary to deal here with two quite different situations. A settlor may wish to provide a house *in specie* for a relative or other beneficiaries, the most common example being the devise or bequest of his house by a testator for his widow. Alternatively the settlement may be primarily to provide income for beneficiaries and the corpus of the settlement may be land subject to leases, pure personal property, or a mixture of each. It is also necessary to consider in some cases whether the settlement is *inter vivos* or by will.

A. "Occupational" settlements

(i) *Choice of settlement*

A comparative survey of settlements under the Settled Land Act 1925 and those taking effect behind a trust for sale is made *ante*, p. 79. It is the view of most practitioners that a settlement upon trust for sale, subject to the consent of stipulated beneficiaries before dealings take place, is the more satisfactory method. Although the trustees have overall control of the trust property the life tenant under the trust may, of course, be appointed a trustee. It is even possible to create entailed interests in the trust property since by section 130(1) of the Law of Property Act 1925, entailed interests may be created by way of trust in personalty. From the fiscal point of view, not a great deal hangs on which of the traditional varieties is chosen, but the following points are worth mentioning:

(a) If the land includes agricultural land, *e.g.* the settlement is of a farm house and farm land, then if improvements are made which attract capital allowances or certain repairs to fixed equipment are made which are revenue expenses deductable from rents or profits for tax purposes, the tenant for life may still recoup these expenses in full from the capital of the settlement (see *Re Pelly's Will Trusts* ([1957] 1 Ch. 1), Settled Land Act 1925, ss. 73(1), 75(2), 83 and 84, and Agricultural Holdings Act 1948, ss. 81(1) and 96(1); however, in *Re Duke of Wellington's Estates* ([1971] 3 W.L.R. 184) the tenant for life of settled land was held to be not entitled to recover sums paid by him to outgoing tenants under the Agricultural Holdings Act 1948, s. 47(1) as compensation for improvements made by them). If the land is vested in trustees for sale, they have a discretion whether to pay for such improvements made by the estate owner out of capital or income, and so those entitled to the income under the trust are not assured of the best of both worlds (see *Re Wynn* [1955] 2 All E.R. 865).

(b) If the property is likely to become dutiable on the death of a life tenant, it was formerly preferable to have a strict settlement rather than an express trust for sale if the land was freehold. This was because the privilege of paying duty by instalments over eight years, with a low rate of interest on outstanding balances was formerly limited to realty. Illogically it did not apply to leaseholds or land regarded as personalty because of the imposition of a trust for sale. This distinction has now been removed, the privilege now applying to any land other than interests therein by way of mortgage or security (F.A. 1971, s. 62).

(c) Whichever method is chosen, the life tenant in occupation is taxable on any sums paid by the trustees in respect of outgoings applicable to the property (*I.R.C.* v. *Miller* [1930] A.C. 222).

(d) The traditional form of settlement is on trust for a beneficiary for life with remainders over. If these remainders include further successive life or entailed interests the passing of the trust fund for estate duty purposes on the dropping off of each life is likely seriously to deplete the capital. There are several ways of avoiding or mitigating this situation even within the framework of the traditional settlement, and they involve making use of exemptions from duty such as the exemption in favour of a surviving spouse not competent to dispose. These exemptions will be mentioned more particularly later. It is possible, though, to achieve the same effect as a short-term settlement by quite another device, namely by settlements for terms of years. Formerly a convenient method was for the "settlor" to grant to the "life tenant" a lease for life at a nominal rent. By section 149(6) the term is converted into one of ninety years terminable after the death of the tenant by one month's notice and no duty would have been payable on the tenant's death. The freehold reversion could also have been given to a second beneficiary. Now by virtue of section 36(5)(a)(ii) of the Finance Act 1969, "settlements" caught by section 2(1)(b) of the 1894 Act include "a lease of property which is for a life or lives ... that property being treated as the property comprised in the settlement." But there would appear to be no reason why the "settlor" should not lease the land to the "life tenant" for a term of years based on his actuarial expectation of life and then dispose of the freehold reversion to other beneficiaries. It is quite possible that the granting of the lease at a nominal rent to the tenant, particularly if the lessee were a relative of the lessor, would be regarded as a gift within section 2(1)(c) of the 1894 Act (see F.A. 1940, s. 44) as would the disposal of the reversion. However, once the period of vulnerability had expired there should be little or no duty on the tenant's death, particularly if the lease is short when the unexpired residue forming part of the tenant's free estate would be of small value. If the tenant survived the period of the lease he would of course be dependent on the person entitled to the reversion granting him an extension in the absence of protection under the Rent Acts. Variations on this scheme can be invented— e.g. to X for a term of years, subject thereto to Y for one year, subject thereto to X for life, which might result either in the life interest vesting in possession if X survived the term of years, or alternatively being disclaimed, or, if X died during the term of years, never vesting in possession at all. No duty would be payable if either the life interest is disclaimed or never vests in possession, the recast section 2(1)(b) only catching interests *in possession*.

(e) Were it not for an anti-avoidance provision, it might be possible to avoid or delay the charge to duty by sub-settlements of beneficial interests. Now, under section 36(6) of the Finance Act 1969, an interest in a subsidiary settlement is treated as an interest in the head settlement; so, on the death of a person entitled to an interest *pur autre vie*, the whole settled property passes unless the interest extended only to part of the whole life interest when only the corresponding part will pass. The same principle applies to assignments of beneficial interests, where the settled property passes on the assignee's death. The test is always the beneficial enjoyment of the property; the title to it, whether by direct limitation under a head settlement, or by a sub-settlement or assignment, is immaterial.

(f) The capital gains tax exemption in respect of dwelling-houses occupied by beneficiaries has been outlined above (*ante*, p. 105).

(ii) Specific estate duty considerations

(a) *The charge on settled property.* We have already seen that settled property is charged under section 2(1)(b) of the Finance Act 1894 as amended and recast in 1969. "Settlement" is defined by reference to settlements within the Settled Land Act 1925, or settlements which would be so if they related to "real property in England or Wales." The exclusive reference to the Settled Land Act 1925 is rather odd, since it seems to exclude property held on trust for sale (see section 1(7) of the Settled Land Act 1925, and " 'Coach and Four Driven Through Estate Duty'—Late Extra" by F. R. Davies, [1971] B.T.R. 121) but the point does not seem to have been specifically taken in practice.

Under section 2(1)(b)(i) property which passes on death includes property which at any time during the period of seven years ending with the deceased's death was comprised in a settlement, and the deceased was entitled to a beneficial interest in possession in that property or as successor to an interest of a beneficiary under that settlement. Also included is the case where the interest in settled property was disposed of or determined before the period of seven years but the deceased was not at all times during that period entirely excluded from possession and enjoyment of the property or from any benefit to him by contract or otherwise.

To take a very straightforward example, suppose X settles land on his son Y for life with remainder to Z absolutely. Ten years after the date of the settlement Y dies. His net "free" estate amounts to £25,000 and the capital value of the land is also £25,000. The normal rule is that all dutiable items must be aggregated together to form one estate. This then attracts duty at progressive rates. Here, the estate is treated as one of £50,000, £11,750 is payable in duty, the deceased's executors being accountable for the duty on the free estate and the trustees of the settlement for the duty on the settled land. Had Y's free estate not exceeded £15,000, the aggregation rule would not have applied (F.A. 1972, s. 120). The duty would then have been nil on the free estate and £2,750 on the settled property. Thus a lightening of the free estate by some £10,000 produces a dramatic saving of duty of £9,000 on the total property passing on Y's death.

Two broad conclusions follow from this. First, because of the unpredictable size of the life tenant's free estate it is not possible to estimate accurately the probable extent of the charge of duty on the land. Secondly, if the capital value of the settled land is high, the minimum charge can be estimated and if this is a substantial percentage of the value of the land, successive passings on death can seriously erode the corpus of the trust fund. Indeed it is likely that all or part of the land might have to be sold to pay the duty, thus destroying the settlor's intention.

The basic problem is, then, how can land be settled so as to avert the possibility of a disproportionate amount of duty being payable? Coupled with this question will go parallel consideration of the possible impact of the other taxes during the currency of the settlement.

(b) Estate duty exemptions

(i) INTER VIVOS SETTLEMENTS. The primary fiscal aim of an *inter vivos* settlement is to lighten the settlor's estate and thus lower the effective rate of estate duty on his death. To achieve this, the settlor may have to survive the completion of the settlement by seven years to avoid a charge thereon under section 2(1)(c), though in the last three years of the vulnerability period there is graduated relief by way of reduction of the principal value of the given property (15 per cent, 30 per cent and 60 per cent in the fifth, sixth and seventh years respectively; F.A. 1968, s. 35).

(1) *Marriage settlements* provide the most commonly used vehicle for achieving this aim. The settlement may be ante- or post-nuptial provided in the latter case that it is made in pursuance of an ante-nuptial agreement. To attract exemption from section 2(1)(c) of the Finance Act 1894 (which would otherwise treat the disposition as a dutiable gift *inter vivos*) the gift or settlement must be *in consideration* of marriage. Section 53(1) of the Finance Act 1963 stipulates that the gift is not so treated if the persons who may become entitled include (primarily) any person other than the parties to the marriage, their issue or any spouse of any such issue. In *Re Park (No. 2)* ([1971] 1 W.L.R. 710) a grandfather's settlement was held at first instance not to be in consideration of the marriage of his grandson when it was clear that the settlor's intentions were the saving of estate duty and benefit to the family generally. The marriage was merely the occasion for, not the consideration for, the settlement. However, their decision was reversed by the Court of Appeal ([1972] 2 W.L.R. 276) holding that the gift was exempt since (1) the gift became the grandson's absolute property on taking effect, (2) it was contingent on his marriage, (3) it took effect immediately on marriage, and (4) it was a gift to one of the parties to a marriage. In view of the fourth factor the gift must be assumed to be in consideration of marriage. By section 36 of the Finance Act 1968, where the gift is made by parent or grandparent to either spouse the exemption is

limited to the first £5,000, and in any other case, to the first £1,000. These restrictions have since 1963 seriously eroded the value of settlements of land on marriage, particularly having regard to current land values. The settlement will be exempt from *ad valorem* stamp duty if exempt from estate duty (F.A. 1963, s. 64) but the settlement will be a disposal for capital gains tax purposes. Income arising from the property will not however be treated as that of a parent-settlor for income tax purposes since the anti-avoidance provisions do not apply to married children, even if still minors.

(2) Another type of settlement which uses a specific exemption comprised in section 15 of the Finance Act 1896 is where by its terms the *property reverts* to the settlor. The principle is that no duty is attracted on the death of the tenant for life if (a) he dies in the lifetime of the settlor, and (b) the property then reverts to the settlor. Since the settlor must survive, this device is more suitable for conferring life interests on elderly relatives. It is a condition of the exemption that the life tenant must not at any time previously have been competent to dispose of the property, *e.g.* if at one time the property was owned absolutely by the life tenant. This exemption may be used by a husband and wife in this way. Suppose H owns but does not reside in Blackacre and settles it on W for life and survives for at least seven years. If W dies first the exemption applies. If H dies first his reversionary interest in expectancy is dutiable, but payment may be postponed until the interest falls into possession (F.A. 1894, s. 7(6)). Payment of this duty would seem to be sufficient to qualify the property for exemption in respect of the wife's death under the "limited interest of spouse" exemption described below. Again, the setting up of the settlement attracts capital gains tax and in respect of the income arising from Blackacre, this will be regarded as still belonging to the settlor since he continues to retain an interest in the settled property for the purposes of section 447(1) of the Income and Corporation Taxes Act 1970. On the death of the life tenant no capital gains tax is payable, but there is no "free uplift" in the value of the asset re-required by the settlor.

He is deemed to have so acquired it at its original base value (F.A. 1971, Sched. 12, para. 6).

(ii) SETTLEMENTS MADE INTER VIVOS OR BY WILL. The "limited interest of spouse" exemption has been mentioned already and is undoubtedly the most widely used estate duty mitigation device. It applies where settled property has borne duty since the date of the settlement on the death of a party to a marriage, or would have done so but for the smallness of the estate or some other relevant exemption, and the other party to the marriage dies without at any time during the continuance of the settlement having been competent to dispose of the settled property (F.A. 1894, s. 5(2) as amended). Though this type of settlement is usually made by will, *e.g.* a devise by T of Blackacre to Mrs. T for her life and subject thereto to T's children (or to such members of a wider class as Mrs. T may specially appoint), it may also be created *inter vivos*, or arise under an intestacy or a court order made under the Inheritance (Family Provision) Act 1938 as amended, or under divorce legislation.

A significant general relief was introduced by section 121 of Finance Act 1972 whereby (*inter alia*), in calculating the principal value of an estate occurring on a death occurring after March 21, 1972 the capital value of property given to or devolving on the deceased's widow or widower is to be disregarded up to a limit of £15,000. This relief covers property in which the deceased was given a life interest, and such property still qualifies for the "limited interest of spouse" exemption. Relief may therefore be obtainable in respect of the property on the death of both parties to the marriage (see F.A. 1972, Sched. 26, Pt. V, para. 26).

B. Non-occupational settlements

Land may be comprised in a settlement where it is but one of a number of assets comprising a mixed fund of pure personalty and land. The intention of the settlor here is that the land should produce income, and, probably, at a convenient time sold. Most probably the land and other assets will accordingly be subject to an express trust for sale since the settled land legislation is inapt for such mixed funds. Where a settlement of this kind is involved, the points outlined when explaining the taxes applicable to settlements generally must be borne in mind. A common example of this type of income producing settlement is the family accumulating settlement under which income is accumulated for (usually) the children of the settlor pending either their reaching a stipulated age or application of the income under the statutory or an express power of maintenance for a child's education or benefit (see precedent in Maudsley and Burn's *Trusts and Trustees*, p. 218).

Common, too, is the discretionary settlement under which the income and/or capital or the settlement is distributable to such member or members of a class of beneficiaries as the trustees should in their discretion think fit. Before 1969 this type of trust had the great advantage that since no beneficiary had an interest in the trust property until the trustees exercised their discretion in the beneficiary's favour, if he was one of a class of at least three beneficiaries no property could be said to "pass" on his death and there was therefore no duty (see *Gartside* v. *I.R.C.* [1968] A.C. 553). Discretionary settlements were brought into the estate duty net in 1969. Since it would have been inappropriate to charge them by reference to the deceased's beneficial interest in possession, a test based on the receipt of income from the settlement was instead adopted. In simple cases the effect of this is easily understood. If X dies after April 15, 1969 and during the seven years preceding his death he receives the whole, or a proportionate part of the income from the settlement, then either the whole or a corresponding proportionate part of the settled property is liable to duty under section 2(1)(*b*)(*iii*) of the Finance Act 1894 (inserted by F.A. 1969, s. 36(2)). If the deceased ceased to be eligible or the property ceased to be settled prior to the deceased's death the seven year period involved is that ending when the deceased ceased to be eligible or the property settled, subject to a starting point of April 15, 1963 at the earliest.

The actual working of these rules can be very complex and the reader must be prepared to study the specialist literature (see *e.g.* "Discretionary Trusts and Estate Duty—The Dutiable Slice" by P. A. Lovell [1970] B.T.R. 220). Two points which affect the management of such a trust must be mentioned. First, it is important to note that the rules can produce arbitrary results where a beneficiary receives benefits and dies having been a member of the discretionary class for a period of less than seven years. Suppose X becomes a member of the discretionary class in 1971 and dies one year later in 1972 having during that year received all the income of the settlement. In this event the entire settled property passes and is dutiable. This is because the settled funds passing on death are defined by reference to the proportion of the income paid or applied for the deceased's benefit during the "relevant period." The "relevant period" means so much of the period of seven years as the property was subject to the trust and the deceased eligible to benefit (F.A. 1969, s. 37(3)). Secondly, where an elderly beneficiary in the trustees' view ceases to be a good estate duty risk, and he has hitherto been receiving benefits, it is better for the trustees to refrain from exercising their discretion in his favour rather than asking him to disclaim his "interest" in the settlement. This is because the income benefits received during the seven years prior to disclaimer must be taken into account up to seven further years from his death (*i.e.* the full dutiable slice passes subject only to graduated relief of a reduction in the value of the slice by 15 per cent in the fifth year, 30 per cent in the sixth year and 60 per cent in the seventh year). If, on the other hand, he receives no benefits, then the dutiable slice will immediately reduce in magnitude as past benefits drop out of account after the seventh anniversary thereof (see example in [1970] B.T.R. 234).

Where a land settlement is drafted with operative discretionary trusts it will normally take effect behind a trust for sale. If the "strict settlement" form is adopted the legal estate must be vested in the trustees as statutory owners under the

Settled Land Act 1925 since there is no tenant for life. (For a precedent of family settlement involving discretionary trusts applicable to a fund including land, see Potter and Monroe, *Tax Planning with Precedents*, 6th ed. p. 141; for a discretionary settlement of a personalty fund, see Maudsley and Burn, *Trusts and Trustees*, p. 224).

C. Estate duty exemptions and reliefs relating to land

Where the subject matter of the settlement passing on death is land, for the purposes of estate duty the following general reliefs and exemptions must be borne in mind:

(i) Where the estate consists of *agricultural land*, duty is charged on the agricultural value of that property at 55 per cent of the estate rate. (The "estate rate" is the average amount of duty payable on the whole estate taking into account the progressive slices. It is calculated by dividing the total duty payable by the net principal value of the estate). "Agricultural land" includes pasture, woodland, farm buildings, mansion houses and land occupied therewith. Any development value is dutiable at the unreduced rate. In the ordinary case of farmland and farm buildings not capable of development, the reduction by 45 per cent in the full rate represents a valuable concession which in practice is not infrequently exploited by trustees and private investors. On the other hand lay trustees of a trust holding farmland have to bear in mind that the complex body of law governing holdings and the practical problems of farm management may in other respects reduce the attraction of farm land as an investment.

A similar relief is given in respect of industrial hereditaments (55 per cent of estate rate).

(ii) Where the estate consists of standing timber, the value of the timber is left out of account for estate duty. Duty is payable only on sale of the timber, and then at the rate applicable to the last estate in which the timber passed, without aggregating therewith the value of the timber. The land on which the timber stands is dutiable, but this will usually be at the reduced agricultural rate. Again, this is an attractive estate duty advantage, but timber estates may be difficult to acquire and for many years may be a low or non-yielding investment.

(iii) Estate duty on real property, leasehold property and property treated as personalty by reason only of being held on trust for sale is payable by eight yearly or sixteen half-yearly instalments starting from one year after the death (F.A. 1894, s. 6 as amended by F.A. 1971, s. 62). This compares favourably with the usual rule that duty must be paid within six months of the death.

4. LAND COMPANIES

Before the Second World War there were often tangible fiscal advantages in holding wealth through the intermediary of a company. In the case of land, this could be sold to a private limited company formed for the purpose in return for an allotment of shares. These shares could be settled on the usual trusts for life or family accumulating or discretionary trusts. By a deliberately poor dividend policy the value on the open market of the shares was depressed. Even if all the shares were vested in a tenant for life, on his death the value of the shares which passed would be far less than the value of the assets they represented, *i.e.* the land. This loophole was met by section 55 of the Finance Act 1940 which substituted an "assets" valuation for the former open market, one where the deceased died with a controlling interest in this type of company. A parallel abuse whereby a shareholder with a nominal shareholding by *e.g.* getting the company to pay him a large salary from its income and securing rent-free occupation of a house owned by the company, thus extracting most of the income from it with nominal estate duty liability on his small shareholding, could substantially avoid estate duty, was met by section 46 of the same Act. The effect of this section is that on the individual's death a slice of the company's assets corresponding to the proportion of its income which he had received or could have taken passes on death, regardless of the size of his shareholding (if any).

The effect of these provisions is in theory at any rate, to do no more than put the man who holds assets through the intermediary of a company in the same position as someone holding the assets *in specie*. In practice, of course, shares of this sort are a good deal more difficult to sell to raise the duty than the whole or part of the land which they represent. Furthermore, since the imposition of corporation tax in 1965, the small private company ("close company"), particularly if an investment company rather than a trading company, has borne a heavy fiscal burden. Not only has its income been subjected to corporation tax but the balance of its income had to be distributed, thus incurring income tax and surtax liability. This effect could be mitigated by retaining a maximum of 40 per cent (in the normal case) of distributable estate income, thus saving surtax and also boosting the capital value of the shares. But if and when this accrual of capital value was realised by sale of some of the shares, the capital profit was subjected to corporation tax at a higher rate than that applicable to an individual's capital gains tax. Although the new imputation system of taxing corporate profits as from 1973 abolishes the discrimination in favour of retaining and not distributing profits (so far as the company was permitted to do so), since property companies, the shares in which are settled, are quite likely to wish to retain a substantial proportion of income, and such retentions are likely to be taxable at a higher rate than the new surcharged rate for income accumulated by trustees, (45 per cent) it is questionable if the new system will confer tangible advantages. So there is in the ordinary case still little attraction in forming a private company to hold land on family trusts apart from the saving of higher rate tax in some cases. Even if the fiscal climate were to change, it must be borne in mind that the management of a company in accordance with the formalities of the Companies Act 1948-67 can involve tiresome and expensive obligations.

5. Terminating or re-arranging the settlement

The devastating effect which estate duty can have on settlements has already been demonstrated (see *ante*, p. 115 *et seq.*). To take a very simple example, a settlement conferring an interest on A for life, then to B for life with remainder to C absolutely would mean that the settled property would have borne duty on its full capital value on the deaths of both A and B, unless the surviving spouse exemption or some other relief or exemption applied, or B died before his interest vested in possession. The rate of duty is also affected by the settled property being aggregated with the deceased's free estate unless this does not exceed £15,000 (F.A. 1972, s. 120).

It is therefore often decided prematurely to determine the trusts, either by agreement of the beneficiaries or with the consent of the court. Trustees proposing to take either course must consider two major problems, namely (1) whether it is possible to terminate or re-arrange legally without the assistance of the court, and (2) whichever method is chosen, whether the termination or re-arrangement would involve acceptable fiscal consequences.

(1) Outline of method and consequences of variations by agreement

A settlement may be terminated if all the beneficiaries are (1) ascertained, (2) *sui juris*, (3) agreed upon the proposed course of action, and (4) have not charged or settled their interests (the rule of *Saunders* v. *Vautier* (1841) Cr. & Ph. 240). Where this is the case, a number of methods are available to terminate the settlement. These include:

(i) *Apportionment of the property between the beneficiaries*

Division of the trust assets according to the interests of the beneficiaries is comparatively straightforward and such schemes have had court approval in the past (see remarks of Lord MacNaghten in *Att-Gen.* v. *Duke of Richmond and Gordon* [1909] A.C. 466, 474). Where the beneficiaries' interests are of unequal extent, *e.g.* where there is a life tenant and two remaindermen, the interests should be evaluated actuarily. The share of an elderly life tenant would therefore be less than a third of the whole. Where the property is land, this will be vested in the beneficiaries behind a trust for sale and they will hold their beneficial undivided shares as tenants in common.

The tax consequences of this type of arrangement are as follows. With regard to the former life tenant, he now becomes absolutely entitled to property which will pass with the rest of his free estate on his death. With regard to the rest of the property in which he formerly had a life interest but which is now vested absolutely in the remaindermen, this is caught by the substituted section 2(1)(*b*) of the Finance Act 1969, if the deceased dies within seven years of the partition. This is because the property had been comprised in a settlement during the period of seven years ending with his death and "the deceased was entitled to a beneficial interest in possession in that property" (*ibid.*). There is graduated relief after four years have expired. As regards capital gains, no capital gains tax is payable on the disposal of an interest under the settlement (F.A. 1965, Sched. 7, para. 13) but, since by virtue of the division, the beneficiaries become absolutely entitled to the settled property as against the trustees, a charge to capital gains tax based on the appreciation in value of the property is exigible under Finance Act 1965, section 25(3). This provision is of general application in the termination of settlements and will not be mentioned further.

(ii) *Enlargement of life interest*

Prior to 1958 it was possible to terminate the settlement with impunity from estate duty by the life tenant purchasing the reversion. Duty was reduced because (a) there would be no double passing of the settled property, and (b) the actuarial value of the remainder would be less than the full capital value due to pass on the life tenant's death. Section 28 of the Finance Act 1958 countered the avoidance device inherent in this scheme and the legislation is now contained in section 38 of the Finance Act 1969. The effect of this section is to add the amount paid for the reversion (known as an "interest in expectancy") to the erstwhile life tenant's free estate as enlarged by the value of the formerly settled property, and subject the total amount to duty if the deceased died within seven years of the purchase, with graduated relief after four years.

(iii) *Acquisition of life interest by remainderman*

This is perhaps the most common method of terminating a simple settlement. The life tenant merely releases his interest to the remainderman by way of gift. Again, the life tenant must survive seven years from the date of termination of the settlement (F.A. 1894, (new) s. 2(1)(*b*)(i)), with the usual graduated relief.

(iv) *Disclaimer*

Although the disclaimer of an absolute interest may give rise to a charge for duty (see *Re Stratton's Deed of Disclaimer* [1957] 2 All E.R. 594) a disclaimer of a life interest before it vests in possession will not be caught, since the new section 2(1)(*b*) only applies to interests in possession or under discretionary trusts.

(2) Unterminable settlements

There are, of course, many cases where a settlement may not be terminated. The beneficiaries may not agree, or may not be ascertained, or may not be *sui juris*. In the case of a life interest, it may be held on protective trusts under which no surrender is possible (Trustee Act 1925, s. 33). Although sometimes practitioners are willing to advise trustees to take a risk and to proceed with termination or variation despite one of the above factors being present (often with such protection as insurance or indemnities from all parties can give) this is always unsatisfactory and may involve serious breaches of trust.

Where a settlement is not variable except by sanction of the court it is important to remember the use of the power of advancement. Section 32 of the Trustee Act 1925 implies a power subject to contrary intention, to advance capital with the life tenant's consent to the remaindermen up to half their vested or presumptive share. In practice this power is not infrequently modified by express provision in the settlement to enable an advancement of more than this fraction to be made. Section 32 is expressly made inapplicable to settlements taking effect under the Settled Land Act 1925, even where the land has been sold and the proceeds invested in personalty. It applies, however, to property held upon trust for sale, and advancements are not precluded where the protective trusts under section 33 apply, nor does consent thereto prejudice the life tenant (*Re Rees* [1954] Ch. 202).

Unfortunately there can be fiscal repercussions where an advancement is made. Firstly, the amount taken out of settlement involves a cesser of the interest of the beneficiary in possession thereof and the advanced fund is therefore dutiable under section 2(1)(*b*) as previously mentioned. With regard to income tax, if the beneficiary obtaining the advancement is an infant child of the life tenant who has given his consent thereto, this is regarded by the revenue as a settlement by the life tenant on his infant child and income arising therefrom will be treated as the settlor-life tenant's under section 437 of the Income and Corporation Taxes Act 1970 (see *ante*, p. 109). With regard to capital gains tax, on the termination of a life interest in possession in all *or any part* of settled property, there is a notional disposal by the trustees of *the whole* settled property (F.A. 1965, s. 25(4)). In order to mitigate the severity of this as regards advancements, the Finance Act 1966 (Sched. 10, para. 1(1)) prevents the charge from operating where an advancement is involved if the property the subject matter of the advancement "ceases to be settled property under the settlement" which is normally the case.

(i) Variations with the sanction of the court

The circumstances in which the court will take jurisdiction to vary trusts where the settlement cannot be terminated or varied by agreement of all the beneficiaries, all being *sui juris*, are fully discussed in general works on the law of trusts (see *e.g.* Hanbury's *Modern Equity*, 9th ed. Chap. 21 and Maudsley and Burn's *Trusts and Trustees*, Chap. 16). It is here only necessary to outline the possible courses available, with variations for tax saving reasons in mind.

(a) *Inherent jurisdiction of the court.* The court may approve a compromise on behalf of an infant beneficiary where there is a dispute (*Chapman* v. *Chapman* [1954] A.C. 429) but this, for obvious reasons, is unlikely to be invoked where the only real issue is mitigation of liability to tax. It also has a "salvage" jurisdiction to sanction breaches of trust, but there must be an emergency (*Re Tollemache* [1903] 1 Ch. 457).

(b) *Trustee Act 1925, section 57(1).* This section implies into every settlement the power of the court to authorise transactions not within the power of the trustees to effect where expedient in the "management or administration" of trust property. The power is thus too narrow to be used for the variation of beneficial interests, though *e.g.* a sale of a reversionary interest pursuant to an order under this section may incidentally save estate duty (see *Re Cockerell's Settlement Trusts* [1956] Ch. 372).

(c) *Settled Land Act 1925, section 64.* The useful jurisdiction conferred on the court by this section, which applies to settled land or land held upon trust for sale (*Re Simmons* [1956] Ch. 125) has already been discussed (see *ante*, p. 66). The section gives power to the court to authorise the tenant for life to effect "any transaction ... which in the opinion of the court would be for the benefit of the settled land ... if it is one which could have been validly effected by an absolute owner."

Variations of beneficial interests so as to reduce liability to estate duty may be authorised (*Re Downshire Settled Estates* [1953] Ch. 218) and the section can be regarded as supplementary to the Variation of Trusts Act 1958.

(*d*) *Matrimonial Proceedings and Property Act 1970, section 4.* Paragraph (*c*) of this section authorises the court on granting a matrimonial decree to make "an order varying for the benefit of the parties of the marriage and of the children of the family or either to them any ante-nuptial or post-nuptial settlement (including such a settlement made by will or codicil) made on the parties to the marriage." Paragraph (*d*) also authorises the extinguishing or reduction of their interests under any such settlement. The 1970 Act widened the courts' powers which had existed for many years. Under the older law it had been made clear that the saving of tax if an order varying a settlement were granted is not a deterrent to use the making of such order (*Thomson* v. *Thomson* [1954] P. 384).

(*e*) *Variation of Trusts Act 1958.* A very wide jurisdiction is given to the court by this Act to approve arrangements on behalf of specified classes of persons who because of infancy or other incapacity cannot consent for themselves. The classes include potential beneficiaries presently unborn or un-ascertained. The arrangements may be such as to vary or revoke all or any of the trusts or enlarge the trustees' powers of management or administration. The trust property may consist of realty or personalty.

The way the court has interpreted this wide jurisdiction has been the subject of extensive commentary (see *e.g.*, Hanbury's *Modern Equity*, pp. 386-393 and the periodical literature referred to therein). Again, only its use for fiscal reasons will be outlined here.

The Act is commonly made use of by trustees and bene-ficiaries wishing to vary the trusts so as to mitigate, in a majority of cases, estate duty, and also capital gains tax or income tax. "Nearly every variation that has come before the court has tax avoidance for its principal object: and no one has ever suggested that this is undesirable or contrary to public policy" (*per* Lord Denning M.R. in *Re Weston's Settlements* [1969] 1 Ch. 223, 245).

The breaking of the trust by a whole or partial division of the capital between the parties is a common variation approved. This is normally to prevent depletion of the capital on the life tenant's death, in which case the remainder-men are bound to benefit by the accelerated receipt of a larger sum of capital. Remaindermen and their issue may alter-natively be benefitted by fresh, widely drafted discretionary trusts. The old type of settlement involving successive life or entailed interests and cross remainders such as those set out in the example on page 23, described in Potter and Monroe's *Tax Planning* (6th ed., p. 263) as "surprisingly com-mon a few years ago," can be varied by eliminating the cross remainders and substituting discretionary trusts for the life interests with an accelerated date for ultimate distribution.

The court's jurisdiction has also been invoked in the most drastic tax avoidance manoeuvre of all, namely, when it is desired to "emigrate" the trust out of the jurisdiction. An English settlement was converted into a similar Canadian one in *Re Seale's Marriage Settlement* ([1961] Ch. 574) in circumstances where the beneficiaries had been living in Canada for some time. A similar decision was reached where the trust was exported to Jersey, the family having lived there for nineteen years, in *Re Windeatt's Will Trusts* ([1969] 1 W.L.R. 692). However in *Re Weston's Settlements* ([1969] 1 Ch. 223) the Court of Appeal refused to sanction a similar application since (*per* Lord Denning M.R.) "the family had only been in Jersey three months" and "the underlying pur-pose was to get there in order to avoid tax. I do not think that this will be all to the benefit of the children," that is "their educational and social benefit." Harman L.J. founded his objection on perhaps less tenuous grounds, namely that Jersey "has never had any experience of trusts and so far as appears, the courts of Jersey have never made an order executing the trusts of a settlement."

6. THE OBJECTIVES AND INCIDENCE OF SETTLEMENTS

It would be misleading to believe that the overriding consideration when framing a modern settlement is necessarily the fiscal consequences of its provisions. There may be many occasions when the more traditional purpose of tying up property behind a trust involving a life interest, or perhaps on protective or discretionary trusts, must still remain paramount. Nevertheless the draftsman if technically proficient must know the varying fiscal consequences of alternative forms of settlement and bear in mind the considerable financial benefit that can be conferred on beneficiaries if estate duty or capital gains or income tax charges can be avoided. The knowledge that lies behind this proficiency is not easy to acquire, nor is the process facilitated by annual and often drastic changes in tax law. Nevertheless, for the reasons explained in this chapter, this knowledge is an essential part of the stock-in-trade of lawyers involved with trusts and settlements.

In view of the fiscal and other attractions of making settlements in appropriate circumstances, it may be asked how common they are. Very little modern empirical research has been undertaken on the incidence of settlements, whether by will or *inter vivos*.

The Land Registry's records which at first might seem a hopeful source of information on the incidence of settlements are in fact not so, primarily because of the policy of registered conveyancing to keep details of beneficial interests off the register. Thus whilst the existence of a trust for sale, for instance, will be revealed by registration in joint names, there will normally be no indication of whether the beneficial interests are successive or not. The beneficial interests are protected by a restriction, but section 74 of the Land Registration Act 1925 prevents the Land Registrar from being concerned with the particulars of the trusts, "which shall so far as possible be excluded from the register." So too, the Index of minor interests set up to record dealings with interests or trusts (see L.R.A. 1925, s. 102) might in theory provide some evidence, but it is now used so rarely (a mere handful of entries each year) that is regarded as obsolescent.

In an article in 1969 67 Michigan Law Review at page 1303, Professor Browder compared patterns disclosed by investigation of 223 testate estates in Michigan and 100 wills in the English Principal Probate Registry in 1963. Of the hundred wills examined, twelve revealed the creation of life interests. "As in Michigan,' 'the author states, "spouses predominate as life beneficiaries" (at p.1349). Similar research undertaken across the Irish sea revealed that the species of life interest known as the "right of residence" was much more common there, particularly amongst the agricultural community (see (1970) Vol. 21 Northern Ireland Legal Quarterly, p. 389).

Despite the small number of wills examined by Professor Browder, the conclusions reached are probably not atypical. Probably between 12 and 14 per cent of wills continue to contain settlements, and many of these would include in the settlement the matrimonial home or other land. A popular alternative to the creation of a life interest in favour of a spouse, particularly where the estate is not large, is an outright gift to the surviving spouse. This is often on the understanding (but without the creation of a trust) that the surviving spouse's will would in turn leave the inherited property to the issue. In the case of smaller estates, avoidance of estate duty is not in issue and there is therefore no *fiscal* purpose served by the creation of settlements. Consequently, if the importance of settlements were assessed not by frequency but by reference to the value of property disposed of on death, it is likely that much more than 15 per cent of the total of property passing by will per annum would be involved.

Similarly, *inter vivos* settlements, though forming a small fraction of the total number of transactions involving land, account for a higher proportion of the total value passing. This is now partly in consequence of the generally given advice that the administrative and other costs involved in creating and running *e.g.* a settlement upon discretionary trusts are out of proportion to the benefits unless the property is worth at least, say, £50,000. In other cases too, though, some lawyers may miss opportunities of tax mitigation by a lack of awareness of all the options open. Only the simple ones tend to be mentioned in the standard books, the more specialised precedent books being less generally used.

7. THE ROLE OF THE LAWYER IN MAKING SETTLEMENTS

It should be emphasised that the belief which now seems to form part of the traditional wisdom that "lawyers have lost out on taxation to accountants" is certainly not true in the case of settlements, whether these be of personalty or land. To take an example from the procedure on the drawing up of a settlement of shares in a family business in order to avoid an assets valuation of the shares on the death of the majority shareholder, this often involves a co-ordinated operation between the accountants to the business, its solicitors and, where necessary, counsel. Both professions have their functions and there is likely to be some overlap. In settlements of land, lawyers are likely to have the predominant role. This topic has estate duty implications, and estate duty involves the application of the law of contracts, trusts, companies and conflict of laws. Accountants do not generally claim to be skilled in the theory or application of all these topics whereas lawyers do. Furthermore solicitors enjoy a monopoly of drawing up most deeds for reward (see Solicitors Act 1957, s. 20) and consequently the execution of the settlement will be the concern of the solicitor. So long as this situation continues (and the modern tendency is to make the study of taxation an important part of the qualifying process in the case of both barristers and solicitors), the lawyer will continue to play in advising the lay client both on the fiscal desirability of a settlement and its implementation.

8. ATTITUDES TO TAX AVOIDANCE

(1) Judges

Having described in some detail some of the advantages open to the draftsman aware of the law as well as some of the traps awaiting those who do not, it is perhaps appropriate to conclude with a brief comment on attitudes to tax avoidance.

The law reports are full of dicta containing judicial reactions to schemes coming before the court involving tax avoidance devices. In most cases whatever the judge's individual views may be, he is bound to proceed on the footing that a scheme validly drawn with the objective of saving tax is effective to do so. The fact that "there is no equity in a taxing statute"—or that a subject may not be taxed unless statutory liability is clearly imposed, leaves him little discretion. Where there is no real discretion, the tax avoidance scheme if regarded as sufficiently serious by the Treasury, will in due course attract anti-avoidance legislation. Some commentators have contemplated an overall "block-busting" provision to remedy this rather piecemeal anti-avoidance policy, such as that applicable in Australia. There, section 260 of the Income Tax and Social Services Contribution Assessment Act 1936-60 runs:

"Every contract, agreement, or arrangement made or entered into, orally or in writing, whether before or after the commencement of this Act, shall so far as it has or purports to have the purpose or effect of in any way directly or indirectly—

(a) altering the incidence of any income tax;
(b) relieving any person from liability to pay any income tax or make any return;

    (c) defeating, evading, or avoiding any duty or liability imposed on any person by this Act; or

    (d) preventing the operation of this Act in any respect,

be absolutely void, as against the Commissioner, or in regard to any proceeding under this Act, but without prejudice to such validity as it may have in any other respect or for any other purpose."

The effect of the very wide spectrum here presented has been, as a general rule, to encourage the judiciary to protect the taxpayer against the undiscriminating nature of the legislation except in somewhat extreme circumstances (see the review of the cases in [1961] B.T.R. 247 and [1971] Annual Survey of Commonwealth Law at p. 294. In any event, the Royal Commission on the Taxation of Profits and Income, Cmnd. 9474, recommended against the adoption of any such measure in the United Kingdom for these reasons:

"The United Kingdom system does preserve the conception that a person's liability to pay taxes should be imposed in explicit terms and with the authority of Parliament. It does make it possible that there should be some informed discussion and criticism of specific proposals advanced by the Chancellor of the Exchequer before they become law. We think that those are advantages of great importance, all the more so because, as we have tried to show, avoidance is not a word of exact meaning or at any rate does not denote an activity which is in all contexts obnoxious. The cost of the present system is represented in part by additions to the tax code that are certainly prolix and sometimes obscure. If it was also represented by any considerable measure of failure to control the progress of avoidance, we think that it might be necessary to suggest a different and more radical approach to the problem on the lines pursued in other countries. But our general impression is that there has not been any failure of this sort" (para. 1026).

In other cases judges may be faced with a true discretion to uphold a particular scheme. This is either because the statute law is ambiguous in its operation or it is otherwise not clear on which side of the borderline a particular scheme falls, or because the scheme is subject of an application for approval under a statute such as the Variation of Trusts Act 1958. The former case necessarily involves statutory construction, and judicial attitudes tend to vary with the political and economic climate. The traditional attitude was expressed by Lord Cairns in 1869:

> "If the Crown, seeking to recover the tax, cannot bring the subject within the letter of the law, the subject is free, however apparently within the spirit of the law the case might otherwise be." (*Partington* v. *Att-Gen.* (1969) L.R. 4 H.L. 100, 122).

In other cases, particularly during the World Wars and also of recent years, the courts have tended to resolve ambiguities against the taxpayer, particularly if dividend-stripping or some other scheme involving a high degree of artifice, comes before them (see *e.g. Latilla* v. *I.R.C.* ([1943] A.C. 377) particularly at p. 381, and *I.R.C.* v. *Land Securities Investment Trust Ltd.* ([1969] 2 All E.R. 430). Secondly, where the court has a discretion to approve, some judicial attitudes have already been discussed in the context of the Variation of Trusts Act 1958 (*ante*, p. 130). However, the rationale of this legislation leaves little room for a judge's disapproval of tax avoidance itself to determine the exercise of his discretion since one of the objects of the legislation was to enable the re-arrangement of beneficial interests to mitigate tax. As Russell L.J. stated in *Public Trustee* v. *I.R.C.* [1965] Ch. 286 at p. 327:

> "If by an adjustment or variation of beneficial interests a small group can avoid contributing, say, £100,000 to the Crown out of their own pockets, they are well entitled to do so. If any moral criticism could be levelled at them,

then the consciences of the judges of the Chancery Division, in the exercise of their discretionary jurisdiction under the Variation of Trusts Act 1958, would be in a sorry state."

(2) Practitioners

It has already been suggested that the practitioner who agree to advise a client cannot withhold the key of knowledge with regard to the means of tax avoidance. It is for the client to decide whether morally he wishes to take advantage of the advice. The Crown is, of course, also frequently advised and represented by barristers in private practice who appear for the Crown in the more important cases.

(3) Lawyers in public

It must be remembered that lawyers play an important part in the framing of and implementation of the tax laws. These are planned and drafted by the combined expertise of lawyers and others in the Treasury and Inland Revenue Department and finally by the Parliamentary Draftsman (see the Statute Law Society's booklet "Statute Law Deficiencies," at pp. 16-17). In parliament, lawyers will play a large part in either helping to present or oppose the current Finance Bill. Private practitioners may also make representations through the professional bodies to the Chancellor, and these have over the years greatly improved the quality and practicability of tax legislation. Blanket condemnation of lawyers *in toto* for their role in tax avoidance, even if this were regarded as morally unjustifiable, can be seen at the least to be unfairly generalised.

CHAPTER 8

REFORMING THE LAW

Introduction

In respect of the Settled Land Act 1925, Sir Arthur Underhill wrote in 1935:

"The greatest testimony, I think, to the draftsmanship of the Act is, that so few cases have been brought into Court for its construction. This, I feel sure, is largely due to the great care with which, while passing through Parliament, it was revised and criticised by a committee under the chairmanship of Lord Justice (then Mr. Justice) Romer, appointed for that purpose by Lord Birkenhead." ((1935) 51 L.Q.R. 252).

Enough has been said about the historical problems affecting "land in fetters" and the way that successive draftsmen attempted to solve the problem (see Chapter 3 in particular) to show that the draftsmen did indeed show great creative skill in their attempts to solve these problems. Nevertheless, volume of litigation is not necessarily the best indication of a satisfactory substantive law in basically non-contentious subjects such as conveyancing. Many difficult problems have arisen, a number of which are discussed in Chapter 6. It has been mentioned earlier (see *ante*, p. 66) that a great deal of academic debate has occurred with regard, in particular, to the present dual system, trusts for sale and strict settlements. (See Maudsley and Burn, *Land Law–Cases and Materials*, p. 179, note 3 for a detailed bibliography, and *ante*, p. 80). It is the purpose of this chapter to look briefly and far from comprehensively at how countries have tried to solve the problem, wholly or partially, and in particular to look at the draft legislation prepared for Northern Ireland

and published in 1971 which is thought to be the most modern attempt to create a new and unified code.

The Commonwealth and Israel

Settlements of land akin to the English strict settlement tend, for historical, social and economic reasons, not to be an exportable commodity and are not commonly found even in the older Dominions. So, too, within the modern Commonwealth, and in the case of some other countries not within but which have adopted a common law system, it is rare to find even that parts of the 1925 English conveyancing legislation have been copied. In Australia, for instance, it is the legislation of the late nineteenth century that has been copied, and in the case of settlements this is either the Settled Estates Act 1877 (*e.g.* New South Wales) or the Acts of 1882-90. The experience there has been that the Torrens system of titles registration has obviated the need substantially to amend the old law along the lines adopted in England. In New South Wales and Victoria, however, entails have been abolished, words of limitation applicable thereto passing instead the whole estate of the grantor. Similarly in New Zealand existing entails are converted into fees simple absolute and the future creation of entails is prohibited (Property Law Act, s. 16).

In Canada, the various provinces have adopted an "in force" date for the reception of English law, subject to amendment or repeal locally. The result, as a Canadian judge remarked, is "that the law of land in countries under the common law of England is a 'rubbish-heap which has been accumulating for hundreds of years, and ... is ... based upon feudal doctrines which no one (except professors in law schools) understands'" (*per* Riddell J. in *Miller* v. *Tipling* (1964) 43 D.L.R. 469, 477). The result is that such statutes as *De Donis Conditionalibus, Quia Emptores* and the Statute of Uses were re-enacted in *e.g.* Ontario. However the estate tail has suffered the same fate as in parts of Australia having been abolished by statute, with varying degrees of thoroughness, in Alberta, British Columbia, Nova Scotia, Ontario and Saskatchewan. The uniformly adopted solution is to deem limitations which would have created estates tail effective instead to create a fee simple or other the greatest estate that the grantor or testator had.

One comparatively recent attempt to legislate for settlements in Africa is worthy of note. This was the state of Western Nigeria's enterprising up-dated version of most of the 1925 legislation in 1959 to replace the old law received as at January 1, 1900. With regard to settlements, which are very uncommon there, the legislature adopted the solution of converting all existing settlements into trusts for sale and making this method the only way possible to settle land in the future (Property and Conveyancing Law 1959, ss. 32-37). Enterprising though this solution is, as worked out in the legislation, it has been the experience of some conveyancers there that a trust for sale in the case where the idea is to retain the land within the family is quite as puzzling a concept to the layman as the other type of settlement. Professor O. R. Marshall in his critique of the Western Nigerian legislation, writes "it would have been simple and more effective for the legislature of Western Nigeria to have adopted the institution of the ordinary trust instead of the trust for sale" ((1965) Nigerian Law Journal, Vol. I, No. 2, p. 153). Kenya in fact conducted a similar experiment much earlier in its Trusts of Land Act 1941, the effect of which is briefly commented on in (1943) 59 L.Q.R. 24. Some other African states, e.g. Northern Nigeria and Tanzania have attempted a more general solution to the problems caused by inheritance of unsuitable English law by in effect nationalising land ownership and limiting beneficial interests to terms of years granted by the government. In Tanzania the court is given specific powers to adjust by appropriate down-grading beneficial interest in settlements of former fees simple (see R. W. James, *Land Tenure and Policy in Tanzania*, pp. 145-147).

Israel has recently passed legislation which at first glance appears to revolutionise the land law by a draconian process of simplification. It started from the position as declared by

Article 46 of the Palestine Order in Council 1922, which states in effect that where the local law is incomplete the rules of common law and equity prevailing in England form a supplementary source. Two recent statutes, the Succession Law 1965 and the Land Law 1969 sever the connection with English law completely. An important provision of the latter is that the only rights in land which are recognised are "ownership," leases, mortgages, easements and "pre-emption." Other rights, particularly equitable rights, are not recognised. However the Succession Law 1965 does specifically envisage the creation of future interests by will, *e.g.* those in a grant to A for life, remainder to B or a grant to A but to B if a contingency occurs (ss. 42-44). Dr. Joshua Weisman of the Hebrew University of Jerusalem comments as follows on this paradoxical scheme and in particular the above provisions of the Succession Law 1965 as viewed in the light of the Land Law 1969:

"The existence of these (future) rights poses the difficulty of how to treat them within the general scheme of land law. Do such rights fit into the list of rights mentioned in the Land Law? What is the nature of the right of an heir before the vesting condition or the divesting condition has been fulfilled? How will such conditional rights be registered in the land register? The impression gained from reading the Land Law is that the legislature did not reckon with the existence of these rights when enacting the Law. The lack of attention in the Land Law to future interests has additional aspects. Why does the Land Law not refer to the possibility of creating *inter vivos* rights similar to those that the Succession Law allows to be created by will?" ((1970) 5 *Israel Law Review* 379, 410).

This seems to show that a policy of simplification by ignoring what people like to do in wills or settlements is unlikely to be satisfactory.

Northern Ireland

The English property legislation of 1925 does not apply to Northern Ireland and except in the area of trusts and administration of estates has not yet been copied in outline or detail. However, a recent Act modernises the law relating to titles registration (Land Registration Act 1970) and this Act was passed as a result of recommendations contained in the report of the Committee on the Registration of Title to Land in Northern Ireland (Cmd. 512 (1967)).

This report ends with some comments on the substantive law and was particularly critical of the law relating to strict settlements, as the following passage shows (para. 141):

"We do not think that the elaborate dual system of settlements, *viz.* the settlement within the Settled Land Act 1925, and the trust for sale under the Law of Property Act 1925, is suitable for Northern Ireland. We incline to the view that there should only be one kind of settlement which might be declared to exist whenever 'land is held in trust for persons in succession or subject to family charges or for the benefit of an infant or of two or more persons beneficially as joint tenants or tenants in common.' (See the article 'Conveyancing and the Property Acts of 1925.' [(1961) 24 M.L.R. 123]). We do not propose to enter into the detailed questions of whether the powers of disposition, leasing, etc., should be vested in the tenant for life, trustees, or in some other person. Our concern is to draw attention to the necessity of ensuring (a) that these important powers are available and freely exercisable *as respects all land put into settlement*: and (b) that the legislation *specifies clearly the person or persons who are to have the powers*. The dual system in England appears to have given rise to some very wasteful litigation in which the issue was whether a particular arrangement was a settlement under which the disposition powers resided in the tenant for life, or a trust for sale with the powers being in the trustees, there being no doubt at all that *someone* had the necessary power.

The fact that under the trust for sale machinery the legal estate continues throughout the relevant period in a set of trustees and their survivors, and has not to be revested from time to time as the life tenant changes, seems to us to be a decided advantage of this type of machinery."

A working party was accordingly set up to review the law, and its report entitled Survey of the Land Law of Northern Ireland (H.M.S.O. 1971) includes a draft Bill dealing in a more modern way with (*inter alia*) the subject matter of the English Law of Property Act 1925 and the Settled Land Act 1925. Part III of the draft Bill deals with settlements (in clauses 22 to 54) and the main provisions will now be outlined.

Basic form

The working party also concluded that a dual system of settlements was undesirable and also rejected the idea of substituting a trust for sale in all cases. This was partly because of agreement with the criticism of the Nigerian legislation along these lines and partly to accord with the views of legal practitioners locally who gave evidence to the effect that the difficulties of explaining the use of a trust for sale to clients were such that settlements tended to be drafted as strict settlements rather than behind trusts for sale.

Accordingly the solution adopted was to recommend that when land is already settled or is in future settled (and in cases of co-ownership) the land will be held upon "the statutory trusts," whereunder the legal estate is held by the trustees who will have all the powers of a beneficial owner except as limited by the legislation. This scheme would not apply, however, if the settlor himself has created or in future creates a trust for sale, in which case the land will, as under the statutory trusts, be held by the trustees upon trust to sell, but with a mere power to postpone sale. In either case the legal estate and the powers relating thereto are in the trustees, but many of the complexities of the strict settlement disappear (and in particular the conflict between the tenant for life's limited ownership but almost absolute powers). In other words flexibility is preserved by allowing either a "static" land-holding trust or a trust for sale. The conversion of settled land into land held upon the statutory trusts (as defined) is effected by clause 34 in this manner:

"Where any land (other than land held upon trust for sale) was, immediately before the commencement of this Act, limited to or in trust for any persons by way of succession or vested in an infant or trustees for an infant, the same is, from the commencement of this Act, held by the trustees in whom the land is at that time vested, or, if none, by the trustees or other persons specified in section 35, on trust to give effect to the rights of the persons to or in trust for whom the land is limited."

Delegation

To meet criticisms given in evidence that such a scheme would take away valuable rights of existing tenants for life pertaining to the control of the land, the scheme includes provision for delegation of powers by the trustees to the tenant for life. The recommendations are that in the case of future settlements the trustees should have revocable powers of delegation to the life tenant of the powers of leasing and management, and that in the case of existing settlements such a delegation shall have been deemed to have taken place irrevocably. Where the initiative to exercise any power comes from the trustees, there is a general duty to consult with, and where possible to give effect to the wishes of, the beneficiaries. None of these details affect the basic scheme— that in all cases the legal estate is vested in ascertainable trustees.

General simplification

Whilst the general principles of the English law of Settled

Land and Trusts for Sale have been preserved (and in particular the overreaching effect of conveyances of trust land is ensured) the fact that the draft legislation is contained in a mere thirty-three clauses without significantly circumscribing the rights of settlors or beneficiaries speaks for itself.

Prospect for reform in England

Nearly fifty years has elapsed since the "New Property Acts" (as they are still sometimes called by elderly practitioners) were passed. Most writers agree that the Acts as a whole have been most successful, but make detailed criticisms and a few suggestions as to more major reforms (see *Megarry and Wade*, "Forty Years On," p. 1126, and (1961) 24 M.L.R. 123). Some reforms of a comparatively minor nature have already been made as a result in some cases of the proposals of the Law Commission (*e.g.* reduction in the statutory length of title and certain other matters in the Law of Property Act 1969, for a stimulating critique of which see the article by S. Cretney in (1969) 32 M.L.R. 477.

Despite the various criticisms that have been made as to reforms in England of the law relating to settlements of land and the general view that the present position is unsatisfactory both as to settlements and the continued existence of entails (see, on the latter point, *Megarry and Wade*, p. 1127), no significant legislative progress towards reform in this area has yet been made. When significant reform does come, it is likely to be on the initiative of the Law Commission. Although the Law Commission has published no proposals as yet, the subject of settlements of land is believed to be on its longer term agenda of matters for consideration. It must at present be a matter of speculation as to whether proposed reform would still seek to preserve the dual system, but with provision against the "accidental strict settlement" not infrequently created by the amateur will draftsman, or whether more far-reaching reform along the lines discussed above would be recommended.

INDEX

147